**W9-ACR-000**

THE DOUGLASS SERIES ON WOMEN'S LIVES
AND THE MEANING OF GENDER

# UNEQUAL
# COLLEAGUES

## THE ENTRANCE OF WOMEN INTO
## THE PROFESSIONS, 1890–1940

Penina Migdal Glazer and Miriam Slater

RUTGERS UNIVERSITY PRESS

New Brunswick and London

Library of Congress Cataloging-in-Publication Data
Glazer, Penina Migdal.
Unequal colleagues.

(The Douglass series on women's lives and the meaning of gender)
Includes index.
1. Women in the professions—United States—History—20th century—
Case studies.  2. Sex discrimination in employment—United States—His-
tory—20th century—Case studies.  1. Slater, Miriam, 1930–
II. Title. III. Series.
HD6054.2.U6G55  1986    331.4'81'000973    86–6568
ISBN 0–8135–1186–0
ISBN 0–8135–1187–9 (pbk.)
British Cataloging-in-Publication Information Available.

To Our Husbands
MYRON P. GLAZER
PAUL SLATER
who support both careers
and marriage

# CONTENTS

# ILLUSTRATIONS

# ACKNOWLEDGMENTS

In the lengthy collaboration that went into this book we were fortunate to receive help from a wide range of people. Each of us received support to develop the book. We are grateful to the Russell Sage Foundation, the Wellesley Center for Research on Women, and the Smith College Project on Women and Social Change. In addition, at various stages Hampshire College provided us with faculty research grants.

Researchers are always indebted to libraries and archivists who make their collections accessible. The staffs of the Sophia Smith Collection and College Archives, especially Eleanor Lewis, Dorothy Green, and Susan Grigg; the Mount Holyoke College Library Archives, especially Anne Edmonds and Elaine Trehub; the Schlesinger Library at Radcliffe College; and the Smith College School for Social Work were endlessly knowledgeable, helpful, and patient and had the gift of making us feel that our work was a principal concern of theirs.

We want to thank Thomas C. Mendenhall for allowing us access to the papers of his mother, Dorothy Reed Mendenhall. Rachel Levine, the literary executor of Bertha C. Reynolds's private papers, kindly gave us permission to quote from them. An earlier version of Chapter 3 appeared in an anthology R. B. Outhwaite, ed., *Marriage and Society,* London, Europa Publications, 1981.

In the process of writing and revising the book, many colleagues and friends gave thoughtful commentary and suggestions that allowed us to refine our ideas and avoid unnecessary errors. Although it is impossible to mention everyone by name, we would like to thank the Feminist Studies Faculty Group at Hampshire College, especially Margaret Cerullo; the Smith College Project on Women and Social Change, especially Susan Bourque and Kay Warren; Joyce Antler, Joyce Berkman, Jill Ker Conway, Mickey Glazer, Michael Lewis, Marcia and Joel Migdal, Charles Page, Gail Perlman, Margaret Rossiter, Joan and Donald Scott, Adele Simmons, Paul Slater, and Frederick S. Weaver. At several important points Mary Roth Walsh was exceptionally generous in helping us clarify complex issues and provided enthusiastic support.

We benefited from the astute editorial skills of Cynthia Lang, and our friend Eleanor Lewis was immeasurably helpful in the final throes of manuscript preparation. Marlie Wasserman and Eileen Finan were generous and helpful editors at Rutgers University Press. Ruth Barton, Ruth Kroon, Bernice Siegel, and Margaret Slater assisted generously with typing and proofreading. Mickey, Josh, and Jess Glazer, and Paul, Margaret, and Leo Slater were always certain that the topic was worth pursuing and consistently offered optimistic encouragement, for which we are very grateful.

# UNEQUAL COLLEAGUES

# THE CONTEXT OF
# PROFESSIONALIZATION

Professional training is a frequent goal of educated women today, despite all the inequities women face in professional life. But the idea that a woman should pursue a professional career was not always accepted with such equanimity. In the late nineteenth century, considerable debate ensued about the proper roles for educated women. Some saw separate women's colleges, medical schools, and law schools as tracks to full professional careers. Others believed that only men should participate in the modernization of the universities and the development of the new graduate and professional schools. However, not all women were content to be excluded.[1]

This book examines four professional fields in their early years, during the late nineteenth and early twentieth centuries, and focuses on the first generation of women to attend graduate schools and receive modern professional training. The early history of professional women needs to be understood as part of a large process of professionalization that occurred in that period; at the same time women's engagement with the professions was very different from men's.[2]

As we shall see, women's aspirations were often received with something short of enthusiasm. Hostility from male colleagues and teachers was not unusual. Family members could show outright displeasure. Dorothy Reed, a future physician, recalled that in the 1890s, "My mother was upset over my plans when I divulged them to her. My great aunts . . . with whom we lived were aghast at the idea of my studying medicine. . . . Medicine was distinctly not a ladylike occupation."[3] To preserve Reed's reputation as a proper young lady during the years she was training at Johns Hopkins Medical School, one of her aunts always explained her absence, discretely, by saying she was "south for the winter."[4]

Even when they became accomplished professionals women continued to face a range of barriers, not least of which was an effort to ignore their genuine achievements and reject their potential as leaders. Dr. Josephine Baker, a leader in public health at the turn of the century, was one of the first—but certainly not the last— woman to face the problem of supervising male subordinates: "It was nothing personal, they assured me, but they could not reconcile themselves to the idea of taking orders from a woman. . . . 'See here,' I said, 'you are really crying before you are hurt. I quite realize that you may not like the idea of working under me as a woman. But isn't there another side of this question?"[5]

The other side of this question is a story that is just beginning to be told. In this study we examine the experience of a small group of women professionals in each of four different fields: college teaching, medicine, scientific research, and psychiatric social work. To understand both the attraction of the professions for women and the roots of prejudice against them, it is necessary to look briefly at the larger context in which both developed.

The modern professions came into being during the excitement and ferment that characterized the rapidly changing, industrializing society of late-nineteenth-century America. From the first, professionals wanted to develop new forms of knowledge and administer the expert services that they expected to control. On the basis of this specialized knowledge they believed that they should control access to the professions and in that way monitor standards of performance. They quickly moved toward the upgrading and lengthening of educational requirements and developed licensing procedures that ensured greater exclusivity. They also formulated an ideology that emphasized not only selection by merit and performance but also service to the community, which presumably eschewed base concern for profit and reward.

This profile of the educated, altruistic, genteel, and implicitly male professional was accepted, rather uncritically, especially among the middle classes. Native-born, white Americans of the middle ranks were unlikely to recoil from or even to notice the class, racial, and sexual biases implicit in this developing ideology. Moreover, early leaders of the modern professions operated in a landscape of burgeoning opportunities for persons of this background. They transformed old occupations and created new ones by shaping new training institutions in the graduate and professional schools, by reordering established work settings such as the hospital, the laboratory, or the social agency, and by attracting public and private support to underwrite solutions to social problems—which with their newly acquired expertise they promised to define and resolve.[6]

The process by which a group of occupations was transformed into powerful and rewarding professional endeavors occurred independently of women's interests. Nevertheless, middle-class and educated women quickly saw the possibilities and challenges of professional life. Understandably, some women of the new middle class saw the emergence of the professions as a historical moment of incomparable opportunity, even as they recognized the formidable obstacles they might have to face. These were unusual women, whose educational experience had enlarged their sense of themselves and expanded their life goals. Born in the decade after the Civil War, these women viewed the simplicities and satisfactions of their mothers' lives as overly tied to private concerns and responsibilities. It was the public world, not a world made up only of family, children, and church, that seemed more compelling to them, especially after the exhilaration of four years of college.

The dramatic shift in values of the post–Civil War years—a time in which everything that had been familiar was now changing—is illuminated in the lives of these pioneers. Even well-placed white, native-born women, now drawn to the drama of new and evolving opportunities, faced a world in flux. Little that they had experienced in their parents' homes had prepared them to meet it.

Imagine a world in which the population was rapidly shifting from a largely rural one, occupied in farming and farm-related activities, to a predominately urban one. Unprecedented numbers of immigrants, many of them newly arrived and strange to the urban environment, tried to find housing in crowded tenements and work in the burgeoning factories, stockyards, and mines.

Most of these new immigrants faced the enormous problems of urban sanitation, housing, and health. Most did not know the English language. The new generation of educated women saw in these slum dwellers both a sad spectacle and an irresistable challenge. The inescapable presence of the poor in every large American city lessened the missionary impulse to go abroad, an impulse that had captured the sympathies and energies of earlier generations of socially conscious women.[7]

If the changes in the larger society were extraordinary, changes in the lives of women were equally marked. These pioneering professionals were among the first generations of college-educated women. They anticipated that going to college would expand their opportunities for advanced education and greater personal autonomy. What they often did not realize was that the benefits of higher education were likely to raise questions about their proper role in society. To a girl just out from under the parental roof, the colleges were heady places, where intellectually gifted women were taken seriously, often for the first time.[8] An alarming number of graduates were sure that they would not go back to their fathers' houses as serviceable maiden daughters or to husbands' houses as helpmates and housekeepers. For example, Dorothy Reed decided to enter medicine "as much influenced by getting into some work that interested me, and being freed from having to live with my mother, and do the sort of things she felt would be likely to make me a good marriage."[9]

As graduates, these women carved out several possible alternatives to marriage. The women in the settlement house movement dedicated themselves to public service and engaged in legislative and political reform, labor organizing, or simply living in the midst of the tenements as neighborly models of middle-class values. For the leaders, this movement became a lifetime commitment, and ordinarily it precluded marriage. Others outside the settlement houses, such as Frances Willard of the Women's Christian Temperance Union, looked to social movements to combine politics, religion, protection of the family, and rights for women. Many of the followers of the WCTU were traditional married women and ardent supporters of domesticity. For the leaders, however, work was the true purpose and involved an alternative to marriage and domesticity. Among the various forms of public engagement for women, one of the most increasingly attractive pathways was graduate training and preparation for a professional career.

Of course, not all college women chose careers over marriage. But emboldened by the relative freedom of their college years, a significant number of graduates rejected or postponed marriage and sought other kinds of living arrangements away from family and kin. Some, such as the pioneer educator M. Carey Thomas, were appalled that "most women's lives were spent in clearing things out of one place to put them in another."[10] They wanted opportunities to be doctors or scientists, professors or social workers, to join the growing group of Americans who felt that they could acquire some special expertise and use it to make some difference in the world.

They knew that the goals of marriage and motherhood were still the accepted ones for women and that marriage and career were presumed to be mutually exclusive. Even the ambitious and progressive professional women thought it foolhardy to try to combine the two. On learning of her cousin Allen Hamilton's engagement to a medical student, Alice Hamilton, by now herself a physician in her mid-twenties, expressed considerable disapproval. In a letter to her cousin Agnes in 1896 she wrote:

> I do think it [is] such nonsense Marian's studying medicine. That is the fault of the transition period in which we live. Girls think now that they must all have professions, just because they are free to, not realizing that the proper state of society is one in which a woman is free to choose between an independent life of celibacy or a life given up to childbearing and rearing the common generation. . . . I suppose she might say that she has a right to follow her own tastes as well as Allen. Well, let her do it then, let her study medicine, but if she practices it simply means either avoiding the burden of maternity or fulfilling its duties imperfectly.[11]

For those who tried to have both marriage and career, the conventional wisdom was clear: they should not expect any degree of success in either, even when they reshaped their goals or lowered their sights. It took extraordinary courage to try to do both in an era when a woman who appeared to fail at motherhood was thought to be not only incompetent, but also immoral. Those who delayed or rejected marriage in favor of careers were made to feel deviant for pursuing what was perceived to be an unnatural set of priorities. Yet many professional women remained single; only a minority married, usually late in life, and they bore relatively few children. Lucy Sprague, the educational reformer, was one of many women who wanted to marry, but feared the loss of her autonomy. In 1911 at age thirty-three, she wrote to her future husband: "If I marry you, your work and your standards shall prevail." She agreed to go ahead with the wedding only after considerable correspondence and reassurance from her future spouse. Her unusual fiancé pointed out that "It is true that we know few married couples who attempt and still fewer who succeed in living thus [as equals], but you and I have certain circumstances in our favor. . . . You would not have to give up your plans, on the contrary you would realize them more effectively by marrying me."[12] This was a most unusual courtship.

WHO WERE THESE WOMEN, PATHFINDERS IN PROFESSIONAL life, who were prepared to overcome prejudice and discrimination and to oppose any efforts to limit their participation in public life to traditional women's roles of church and charity volunteer? If an early camera portrait had been taken of the nine women who provide the major documentation for this study, little would distinguish them from thousands of other women of that era. The group, composed of Mary E. Woolley, Nellie Neilson, Bertha Putnam, Dorothy Reed Mendenhall, Anne Walter Fearn, Florence R. Sabin, Alice Hamilton, Mary C. Jarrett, and Bertha C. Reynolds, were all native-born Protestants. Except for Bertha Reynolds, the social work leader who was born in 1885, they came of age in the last decade of the nineteenth century. Seven of the nine went to eastern women's colleges; only Alice Hamilton, the pioneer in industrial medicine, and Mary Woolley, the president of Mount Holyoke College, graduated from coeducational universities. Although the women came from many sections of the country, most were from the East and none was from the Far West. Florence Sabin, the eminent scientist, was from Colorado, and Anne Walter Fearn, a physician, came from as far as Mississippi, but even they went East to school. The women ranged in wealth and status from Anne Walter Fearn and Bertha Putnam, the distinguished historian, who were from affluent families, to Bertha Reynolds, who came from comparatively modest circumstances. Generally speaking all were from what can be characterized as the new middle class, a loose designation used to describe a range of middle-income people of that period.

What truly distinguishes these nine women as a group is a set of attitudes and beliefs. Whatever the differences in the work they chose, these were persons of extraordinary energy, willing and able to use their gifts, including the virtue of unusual stamina, in the projects they carved out to prove their professional worth. Anne Walter Fearn ministering to the sick peasants of China, or Nellie Neilson and Bertha Putnam searching the history archives of cold, dank British libraries, or Mary Jarrett heading up the Social Service Department of a busy state psychiatric hospital—they all worked with undiminished enthusiasm in the belief that their disciplined, superhuman effort would lead to significant social betterment. Some, like Mary Jarrett, the psychiatric social work pioneer, were founders of new, advanced educational programs for women; all attended graduate school and believed passionately in the importance of these new credentials. Most held the highest degree available in their fields, usually an M.D. or Ph.D. Mary Jarrett and Bertha Reynolds, leaders in social work, were exceptions because they finished their training before a graduate degree in social work was available. Without graduate degrees themselves, they were instrumental in forging graduate programs in social work and fought to make the graduate credential available to future generations of social workers.

Not surprisingly, in this group of nine ambitious women, all were prepared to depart from conventional expectations of family life and only two married. Even the two who married did so when they were in their thirties. Anne Walter Fearn, who went to work in China, had only one child, who died as a youngster. Dorothy Reed, a physician in Wisconsin, also had children, but resumed a public life while two were still quite young.

Ambition, intelligence, and hard work were the qualities that the middle class had elevated to a sacred ideal by the end of the nineteenth century. They were also thought to be the central components for professional success. By these standards, the women we are about to meet should have been among the most eligible to compete for places in the emerging and increasingly exclusive professions. Not only were they white, native born, and college educated, they were also imbued with the same commitment to notions of merit and the importance of scientific training as their brothers and fathers.

There was no shortage of highly trained and capable women among the aspiring professionals of the late nineteenth and early twentieth centuries. In fact, there was always a reserve pool of ambitious and achieving college graduates, with a well-developed sense of entitlement, prepared to surmount whatever barriers were erected to block them from graduate and professional schools. The early period of professionalization cast up a spectrum of professionally trained women whose numbers and variety would not be matched for another half century. There were women whose contributions were at the upper rungs of achievement in an impressive range of fields.

By now it is a commonplace that women faced serious discrimination as they tried to move in these arenas. Systematically, they were paid less, advanced more slowly, and regarded with less esteem. The discrimination they faced was not always obvious. Beyond the outright exclusion that kept them out of certain graduate and professional schools, they also confronted more subtle barriers, which did not necessarily arise as a result of acknowledged and articulated planning and were therefore even more difficult to predict, anticipate, and overcome. In many instances no special policy excluded women from professional possibilities. Decisions to offer most appointments to men and to pay women less, promote them more slowly, and exclude them from eligibility for grants or from editorial boards of important journals were as a rule neither deliberate nor articulated policies. But they occurred with persistent regularity, and their exclusions had profound consequences for professional women.

In trying to sort out the reasons for professional women's successes or failures, it is far too facile to say that there were prejudices against women that they had to overcome. The ways in which the prejudice manifested itself were extremely complex and insidious.[13] Beginning at the end of the nineteenth century and with increasing momentum during the first three decades of the twentieth, significant social and cultural changes affected the emergence of professionalism; more significant for this study, the changes affected men and women differently.

Insistence on notions of merit and service as the hallmarks of professional activity meant that middle-class white men who were competent and acquired the right credentials could ordinarily expect the kind of fair evaluation that led to further opportunities and rewards. Women of this class believed, understandably, that an equal commitment to merit, to meeting the standards, on their part would achieve similar results. After all, would not their accomplishments and work speak for themselves?

Their experience proved otherwise. Even exemplary performance itself did not escape the differences of gender. In men, the drive for success was lauded as healthy ambition; in women, it was disdained as unfeminine. Male physicians were praised for treating either sex; female physicians were accused of unnatural desires if they were willing to examine a male patient. Certain men were seen as natural leaders; in women, leadership was always unnatural, especially if it meant supervising men. These attitudes were not easily compartmentalized. They permeated all areas of professional life and had a direct bearing on advancement, which itself depended on continual assessment and evaluation during training and beyond.

Exclusion and differential treatment of women were reinforced by the strong societal assumptions about women's place in the home. Everyone knew who was supposed to inhabit the domicile, greet the family's breadwinner after an arduous day, foster and enhance his private life with a view toward his public success. A man's professional image required that he be efficient, objective, and devoted to service. There was a strong belief that this kind of absorption in one's career necessitated a separation from domesticity. The middle-class wife was to serve as the unemployed helpmate at home.[14] As professional success was increasingly predicated on character, on the presentation of self as "the model of the gentleman"[15] as much as on expert knowledge, it became increasingly difficult for a woman to carry out that role.

THESE VALUES AND PATTERNS OF BEHAVIOR FORMED PART of the social context for the middle class in the last half of the nineteenth century. Although many ideas about men's and women's proper roles predated the rise of the modern professions, they quickly became central to the formulation of professional ideology. Not only did professionals, like other middle-class men, believe that women should stay at home, they also defined professional behavior in terms that supported and even required this division of labor by sex. Successful professionals were objective, competitive, individualistic, and predictable; they were also scornful of nurturant, expressive, and familial styles of personal interaction.[16]

Women faced the following situation: opportunities for professionals were expanding, yet for women they were circumscribed by a set of prejudices that threw up serious obstacles. As determined, aspiring professionals, women were not easily deterred. They found a variety of ways to respond to the discrimination they faced. As we examine four of the professions in which these women worked, we will find that certain strategies recur as favored mechanisms for career management. For purposes of analysis we have grouped these strategies into four categories: superperformance, subordination, innovation, and separatism. Women often shifted from one strategy to another, depending on the particular circumstances they were facing. Although the strategies are not totally separable and often overlap, they offer a way of looking at the texture, the range, and the limits of the possible in these women's lives.


THE FIRST GROUP OF PROFESSIONAL WOMEN, WHICH WE discuss in chapter 2, consisted of female academics in single-sex colleges who attempted to create separate communities where professional women could live and work. These institutions turned out to be significant for female scholars because they were among the few places that provided continuous employment for women intellectuals. Not only did they offer opportunities for faculty career advancement, they were also deeply committed to training future generations of female scholars.

Our examination of Mount Holyoke College and its history department documents the extraordinary nature of their achievements. When Mary Woolley became president in 1901, she upgraded the academic standards by replacing teachers hired for their moral virtues and strength of character with newly trained Ph.Ds recruited for the quality of their scholarship and their teaching potential. Gradually, the faculty she employed created an environment in which superperformance was highly rewarded. A number of the Mount Holyoke faculty earned reputations as internationally recognized scholars.

In these separate enclaves women academics were easily able to adopt and pursue the professional standards and styles set by their male colleagues at the leading universities. But to do so women adopted personal life-styles very different from male academics. Professors such as Nellie Neilson and Bertha Putnam rejected marriage as incompatible with serious scholarly achievement for women. Both Neilson and Putnam were educated at Bryn Mawr, a leading institution in the training of female scholars. Having earned their Ph.Ds under foremost historians of the time, they were caught up in the excitement of the new scholarship and determined to build an academic department where new scholarly history would replace the more sentimental, moralistic history that had prevailed at the college. Furthermore, Neilson, Putnam, and their colleagues actively sought ways to encourage future generations of scholars who would be willing to set the same priorities and reject marriage in favor of the scholarly life. In the short run, this strategy was successful; it produced a generation of like-minded and successful protégées. In subsequent generations, however, this mission would be vitiated by a resurgence of conventional goals for women's training and employment.

In chapter 3 we examine the case of medicine, a profession dominated by men and developed in the late nineteenth and early twentieth centuries in large part to ensure its practitioners high prestige and control over a wide array of health services. As the power and prestige of the profession unfolded, the barriers against women were reasserted with renewed vigor and grew to massive proportions. Most of the women's medical colleges closed; the new medical schools were reluctant to admit and educate more than a few women. Such prejudice could ordinarily be overcome only by the most ambitious superperformers. One of these, Dorothy Reed, was part of the small, determined number of groundbreaking females who used extraordinary achievement as a lever to maneuver themselves into the newly emerging modern medical schools based on laboratory training and into internships, where they received the finest education then available. In contrast, Anne Walter Fearn received her training in a women's medical college. Most of the women's medical schools and training hospitals were rapidly disappearing or merging with larger men's schools. Fearn's alma mater, the Women's Medical College of Pennsylvania, still remained an important training ground for a number of aspiring physicians.[17]

These two women are part of a small group in this period who chose to marry and have children as well as to pursue professional careers. Their numbers are few, and these two were not typical. But an examination of their lives offers a close look at the inextricable links between professional and domestic life. Both Reed and Fearn are excellent examples of married women taken less seriously by their colleagues because of the widely held assumption that having husbands and children automatically lessened women's commitment to professional goals.

Even after Reed and Fearn proved their dedication and competence to other professionals, they had to resolve additional complications in their own marriages. As members of a tiny minority, they found it virtually impossible to challenge the traditional definition of the role of wife and mother. They had internalized the prevailing cultural assumptions that they should manage household and children without deviating from high standards of performance, even if they were also trying to juggle complicated and demanding careers. Standards at home were set by women whose energies were exclusively channeled into family matters; at work, the standards were set by men whose own wives not only saved them from the distractions of the household, but also provided a home that served as a refuge from the demands of the profession, a "haven in a heartless world."[18] Under these circumstances, superperformance must have seemed a possible strategy only for women of outstanding ability, ambition, and stamina. Even so, superperformance alone was not enough.

Faced with formidable prejudices and conflicting expectations, these physicians expanded their repetoire of responses to include other strategies. When children and family responsibilities precluded a regular practice, Reed and Fearn both found innovative ways to provide different kinds of health services that took them out of active competition with most male practitioners and meshed better with their other responsibilities. Even so, they both experienced lifelong feelings of guilt and ambivalence, and these frequently led to tensions between them and their husbands.

The third profession, research science, the subject of chapter 4, eventually became male dominated, but developed differently from medicine. At the turn of the century, research science was a new field and scientists were still not certain that they could actually earn a living doing full-time laboratory research. This lessened the competition considerably since many men were reluctant to pin their careers on such vague prospects. As wealthy industrial capitalists began supporting modern laboratories, funding for research gradually became more accessible and opportunities expanded. Because those who were prime movers in starting laboratories wanted to prove the worthiness of these efforts, principles of meritocracy were applied with greater seriousness than in the more established fields such as medicine and law. Laboratory directors were eager to have the best scientists so that they might quickly produce startling results that would impress both the public and the funders. They were less interested in the gender or ethnicity of the researchers and more interested in supporting those researchers who appeared capable of producing results.

In this atmosphere women used a variety of strategies to secure places for themselves. Like many other professionals, they turned first to superperformance, which they believed would be the most successful strategy in a field so committed to meritocracy. Despite such a promising beginning, and the eagerness with which they entered this new field, women soon found themselves clustered in the assistant and middle-rank positions in a hierarchy that was increasingly male. Men were chosen to occupy the upper leadership ranks and direct the laboratories, where most women worked as subordinates.

Our study examines the Rockefeller Institute for Medical Research, a major medical research institute founded in 1900 and an institute where women had some initial success. Yet only a few token female scientists made it to the top from what had been a relatively substantial pool of candidates. Florence Sabin, whose life we report in some detail, did indeed become one of the outstanding laboratory scientists in the United States. Her own success, coupled with her inability to maintain openings for future women scientists, demonstrates the limits of even the most outstanding tokens. Alice Hamilton, her contemporary, chose a very different kind of research. After a short career as a bacteriologist, she became concerned with industrial diseases, particularly lead poisoning, and began conducting surveys to establish links between the work environment and disease. Her career, like that of Sabin, culminated in acceptance in high places—for example, Harvard Medical School—but she too was unable to meet even her modest goal of opening the medical school to women students.

Within a few decades, a field that initially seemed to hold much promise for women was highly segregated by sex. Women worked in a few areas, largely as research associates or assistants. Increasingly, the cultural belief grew that women were not very good at science, and the number who studied for the Ph.D. decreased.[19] Only in women's colleges did the tradition of science as a possible career for women continue. For some scientists, physicists for instance, these colleges offered the only possibility of employment beyond the assistant or subordinate level.

In our fourth and final case, psychiatric social work, in chapter 5, we encounter a field that had had a long tradition of female participation. Earlier, social work had been an unpaid volunteer activity that did not require special training. Mary Jarrett and Bertha Reynolds, early leaders of the Smith College School for Social Work, joined a group of women and men who wanted to found a graduate school exclusively for female students. This early group of ambitious professionals understood that control over expert knowledge and the awarding of special credentials was a crucial component of professional autonomy. These innovators self-consciously wanted to create a new profession that drew on an earlier tradition of women's charity work as "friendly visitors," while separating itself from amateurs by emphasizing the scientific knowledge and advanced training that seemed to be the key to success in a separate profession for women.

The social workers never completely succeeded in achieving the kind of autonomy that they hoped control of a graduate institution would bring. They could not free themselves from domination by medical superiors. Whether working in hospitals, clinics, or social agencies, they found themselves subordinate to psychiatrists. Further, innovators such as Bertha Reynolds found that some of the most radical new ideas about psychiatry, which they had fervently hoped would improve the condition of humanity, came to be used as mechanisms of social control. In addition, clinics and social agencies required the support of philanthropists and political leaders. These conservative funders were willing to support efforts to help the poor adjust and become compliant clients. But when social workers began looking at structural rather than personal causes of social problems, they often found themselves at odds with their employers. Social workers did achieve considerable success in creating an important paid profession that remains dominated by women to this day; at the same time a review of their accomplishments reveals the limits of their ability to create a profession equal in power and status to those such as medicine, which they so admired and tried to emulate.

In each of these fields, then—academia, medicine, research science, and psychiatric social work—women achieved some victories and faced a constellation of obstacles because of their gender. These four case studies taken together document a range of different professional possibilities for women and were selected for that reason. Mount Holyoke, a woman's college, offered academic women the experience of a separatist female enclave in which women controlled the immediate institutional setting, if not the profession at large. In contrast, medicine, by the early decades of the century, was a male-controlled profession with formidable barriers against women and other outsiders. Scientific research afforded still another path in a new profession offering equal access, at least in its early development. Lastly, psychiatric social work was also a new profession, but one that established advanced training programs aimed at preparing qualified women for a predominantly female profession. As the women professionals maneuvered to build the best careers possible, they continued to believe in the efficacy of professional life, in the worthiness of that calling, and in the ideology of merit that was so closely associated with all professional work. Women banked so heavily on merit—the belief that if only they were good enough, trained enough, committed enough, their achievement of superior performance would be rewarded—because it seemed so incontestable. Merit and achievement were, presumably, a matter of personal control and volition, and therefore, protected from political manipulation by others.

But as we shall see they had to face the fact that no matter how meritorious their actual performance, women continued to be largely excluded from ranking positions within the professions, positions that controlled access to the resources of the field and controlled recruitment of the next generation. The inability of women to create "progeny"—to safeguard positions for the next generation—meant that many of their hard-won gains could be easily erased. In some cases they were able to develop regional, informal networks that helped pressure the professional organizations to open more opportunities. Where this was not possible, even the most extraordinary achievers remained tokens unable to further the drive for equality. Similarly, their limited numbers in decision-making positions tended to narrow their participation in the creation of knowledge and expertise, the hallmark of professional achievement.[20]

To the extent that these higher reaches of the profession were open to men and not to women, women's chances for equality were diminished. Although the patterns differed in the individual occupations, the experience of the first generation of professionals too often led to marginality: they were opposed in their pursuit of the top rank and were frequently shunted to the side. Their responses, while often creative and proof of the viability of women in professional life, were not enough to overcome their unequal status. To understand how this happened in each of four very different professions, we turn now to our case studies. These nine comparative biographies allow us to analyze with greater precision the nature of inequality in professional life and women's response to the discrimination they faced.

# PROFESSIONAL SCHOLARS IN ISOLATED SPLENDOR

Nothing appeared to offer women more professional promise at the turn of the century than the possibility of completing the requirements for a degree in one of the expanding Ph.D. programs. Although women clearly faced barriers in the admissions process and in the awarding of fellowships for prestigious programs, they were, nevertheless, able to participate in graduate work in relatively significant numbers. The first woman Ph.D. received her degree in 1877 from Boston University. Less than fifty years later, over fifteen hundred women held this coveted degree.[1]

The Ph.D. was sought primarily by persons who wished to teach and do research in colleges and universities, although a small percentage found employment in social agencies, hospitals, businesses, and other organizations. For women, college teaching was a logical extension of elementary and secondary school teaching, fields in which they had already established a major presence. But doctorates were mainly held by men and were more prestigious than other teaching degrees.

Between 1900 and 1920 approximately 10 percent of all Ph.D.s awarded in the United States were granted to women. In the next two decades that figure rose to 15 percent before beginning a thirty-year decline. The proportion of women Ph.D.s who received their degrees from prestigious institutions was the same as the proportion of men Ph.D.s who earned their degrees from top-ranked institutions. The acquisition of the

Ph.D. became attractive to women because it offered new potential for high-prestige, professional employment, especially by the emerging women's colleges.[2]

The women's colleges are particularly important to our study because they were the only reliable source of employment for female scholars and academics. Male and coeducational institutions rarely appointed women to the faculty; when women were given faculty rank, it virtually always carried an adjunct or inferior status.[3] Women's colleges in the early decades, by contrast, were particularly receptive to inviting women to join their ranks. The colleges were attractive to women because they provided an intellectual environment sparked by a sense of mission and possibility for advancement and leadership within the community. In addition, the leaders of these colleges formulated and espoused an ideology that made intellectual life both a legitimate enterprise and an acceptable activity for women scholars. In these efforts, the administration and senior faculty were successful in creating a distinctive environment.

In this chapter, we focus on professional separatism and its impact on the careers of women. To do this we examine the Mount Holyoke College faculty, and particularly the Department of History, because it was one of the most successful manifestations of the professionalization of female faculty.

The development of a women's community of teacher-scholars challenged in profound ways contemporary notions that women should remain in the private sphere. Those who joined the faculties of women's colleges found themselves living in a special style of community that fostered an intellectual life and facilitated career aspirations. Mount Holyoke did more than provide jobs for women. These positions were accompanied by living quarters, food preparation, and a strong reference group that reinforced professional values.

Despite its stunning successes, there were severe limitations to this model of professional separatism as a long-term solution to women's ability to control their private lives as well as have flourishing careers. The Mount Holyoke experience reveals both the strengths and the weaknesses of this professional path as it emerged over several decades.

## MOUNT HOLYOKE: CREATING A SEPARATIST INSTITUTION

Mount Holyoke College was founded in 1837 as a seminary for young ladies, fifty years before the modern academic profession emerged. Mary Lyon, the founder, was one of several pioneers in education in antebellum America. Her ideas about education for middle-class women became increasingly accepted over the course of the next half century. In the 1890s a major change occurred in Mount Holyoke's orientation when the school was chartered as a college and geared up to offer a full college curriculum. This decided shift from the nineteenth-century faculty of pious, Christian ladies to the twentieth-century faculty of productive scholars and intellectuals reflected both social and intellectual developments in higher education generally, as well as the de-

## PROFESSIONAL SCHOLARS IN ISOLATED SPLENDOR

liberate and specific policies of the Mount Holyoke administration.[4]

Although a number of changes had taken place before her accession, the appointment of Mary E. Woolley as president in 1901 marked a crucial break with the past and the rapid reformation and transformation of the teachers into a self-consciously professional faculty.[5] It was also under Woolley's tenure that the professional impulse flourished most fully; Mount Holyoke ceased to be merely a school for girls and became instead a community of women scholars. This new devotion to faculty excellence and achievement marked Mount Holyoke, and the women's colleges that adopted similar priorities, as special institutions for women professionals.

Mary Woolley, born in 1863 in New England, was the daughter of a Congregational minister and social activist who was responsible for her decision to enroll at Wheaton Seminary in 1882–1884.[6] Wheaton, at that time, was one of the new women's seminaries (later to become a college) filled with a sense of mission about the possibilities for women's education. Mary Woolley went on to become the first woman to enter Brown University (1891) and in 1894 was one of the first two women awarded a B.A. She stayed on at Brown to earn a master's degree under the distinguished historian J. Franklin Jameson.

Her formal education ended, Mary Woolley joined

Opposite: Mary E. Woolley at Mount Holyoke. Courtesy of Mount Holyoke College Library/Archives.

the Wellesley College faculty where she rose through the ranks and served as department chair. Her plans for further graduate study never materialized because she was offered the presidency of Mount Holyoke College—a position she held from 1901 to 1937.

Woolley did not hold a doctorate, but that never diminished her belief that the key to building an excellent institution was to raise the standards for faculty. Throughout her career in college administration she also supported a variety of student reforms designed to increase the independence and capabilities of women. She increased the amount of physical education required of students to reinforce the feminist assertion that education of women does not necessarily lead to physical decline. She endorsed student self-government and an honor system when these were still educational experiments rejected by conservative leaders.

Mary Woolley supplemented her work at the college with participation in national affairs. In this Progressive period she supported a variety of reforms and served on many boards in support of labor, in defense of Sacco and Vanzetti, on behalf of suffrage. She wrote and spoke frequently on pacifism. In 1932 she was the first woman appointed as a United States delegate to an international conference on arms control and reduction.

President Woolley had made her intentions clear almost as soon as she arrived at Mount Holyoke, causing some consternation among those who were unprepared for her determination to move as rapidly as possible toward the new professional standards of the best universities. The change in leadership and goals was embodied in her early announcement that the Ph.D. degree was to become a requirement for continued faculty status. Not everyone approved of this standard. One former Mount Holyoke history professor recalled the early response to Mary Woolley's presidency. Prof. Viola Barnes's recollection vividly illustrates the radical disjuncture between the two worlds—the new one of professional scholarship and the older tradition of character building and pious education. Barnes described the reaction of one colleague who believed that Woolley's arrival evoked "a time of disillusionment, hardship, and despair." This colleague complained to a friend that

> Here we were and were proud of it. We kept the ideals of Mary Lyon which were that you could not live by knowledge alone, you had to live by a pattern of Christian womanhood. . . . The emphasis was put on that. All of us, we came raw and untrained—as much to train our characters and prepare us for leadership in the world as Christian women as to learn something about chemistry or Greek or something else . . . the idea was—the earlier chief executives and faculty agreed—that you couldn't do better than to take someone hot off the griddle who'd been trained to it all. Therefore, if there were any vacancies in the faculty, at the end of the year, they invited back the girls they thought most highly of not only for their grades but for their character. And they were appointed. . . . Our job was to carry on. . . . Miss Woolley's first announcement was that all the members of the faculty who had not had any graduate work had their choice: they must either take a leave of absence and go away and take graduate work or resign.[7]

Barnes, in reporting her understanding of Mary Woolley's early policies, went on to add her own interpretation of these demands.

PROFESSIONAL SCHOLARS IN ISOLATED SPLENDOR

> [Mary Woolley] had a new contention of education which
> was for scholarship. Christian womanhood in her mind
> was all right but its importance was immediately taken over
> by the conception of scholarship. This college, if it was
> to last, must develop a reputation for scholarship, and
> scholarship just as good as any men's college offered a man
> . . . and she tried to explain that to them and she made
> them do it.[8]

Requiring advanced degrees was not, of course, some
idiosyncratic notion on the part of the young president.
It was in keeping with the upgrading of standards among
the most competitive men's colleges. Mary Woolley was
determined to create mechanisms to promote the kind
of intellectual activity that the new educational leadership of the country deemed necessary. She had clearly
embraced professional beliefs in merit and in the value of
scholarly research. Later she went well beyond requiring
advanced degrees: she went to great lengths to persuade
the board of trustees of the need to support ongoing development of the faculty, and she took considerable personal interest in helping faculty members find financial
support for their research. By the time she wrote her
1905 Annual Report of the President, she was already arguing for sabbaticals as essential requirements for faculty and pointing out that the "importance of these 'sabbatical years,' so-called, is very great. The profession of
teaching is exhausting, mentally as well as physically,
and an instructor, in order to do her best work, must
stop and be re-created."

The president was equally clear in her goals for faculty development. She wanted some opportunity for personal renewal for her faculty; she also was concerned that they avoid becoming parochial in outlook and isolated from the intellectual currents of the time. The teacher, she continued, "needs to become again a student, not only that she may come into touch with the progress made in her own line of work, but also to gain a broader outlook, that education which is to be found in studying under the men and women who are making history in the literary and educational world."[9]

Mary Woolley seems to have understood that the future of the college was inextricably linked to the reputation of the faculty. She tried to press that view on the board as well as on the faculty and other administrators by reminding them that "It is for the interest of the College, as well as for the individual, and there should be a fund of which the income could be used for the continuance of part salary to members of the Faculty who have been granted leaves of absence for study."[10]

In offering salaried sabbaticals, requiring the doctorate and further publication for advancement, and expecting active pursuit of research and professional activity, Woolley was following the standards that the major men's universities had begun to demand of their faculties. These were the central components that transformed college teaching from a traditional calling to a modern profession. Harvard granted its first sabbaticals in 1880, and the idea began to be copied elsewhere within the next decade. By 1905 presidents of the major universities, in the Association of American Universities, had declared that research was "a major concern of their institutions, thus officiating," in the words of their historian, "at a semi-official wedding of investigation to the older purpose of useful vocational training."[11]

## THE SPECIAL DEMANDS OF FEMALE EXCELLENCE

Mary Woolley understood that faculty women were unable to pursue professional lives and conventional private lives at the same time. For faculty who chose, like her, not to marry, the college would become both workplace and home.[12] The college responded to this unusually large number of single women by continuing to serve as a residential institution for the faculty as well as for the students. Instructors lived in special faculty apartments with a living room and bedroom. Small communal kitchens were provided where each teacher was allowed to prepare one meal a day. A minimum of two meals had to be taken in the faculty dining room, and curfews were strictly enforced for faculty as well as for students.[13]

These arrangements had several consequences. Women were freed from the domestic obligations and chores that traditionally consumed so much time and energy. They enjoyed access to a community of scholars who served as both friends and a reference group for ambitious professionals who were bucking the tide of society. Resisting conventional expectations of marriage and domesticity, they were following in the steps of the brave and scattered few at women's colleges and women's medical institutions. These were women determined to develop a crucial redefinition of the public and private sphere.[14]

Late-nineteenth-century women often developed close, intense relationships with female friends. For professors who were living with neither husbands, parents, nor siblings, these friendships often developed into long-term quasi-familial relationships. In remembering her early days on the faculty, Viola Barnes, who was appointed in 1919, recalled:

> I was struck, when I first came here, that the whole place was divided up by couples. This couple lived in Mead, this couple lived in Porters . . . the two Dotties, Dorothy Hahn and Dorothy Foster, Putnam and Ball, Stokey and Starr and so on. All the way through, the faculty were in twos and I never heard any criticism of that at all. And there was never any idea of the current present twentieth century connotation that is unpleasant.[15]

The faculty's tendency to find special friendships supportive and necessary for the texture of their private lives reinforced the separatist qualities of the college. Mary Woolley's conception of women's possibilities was enacted in her own life and in her vision of Mount Holyoke College. She never married, but shared a close friendship with Jeanette Marks which lasted for decades. For all intents and purposes Miss Marks was family. The two lived together for most of their adult lives, and Jeanette Marks cared for Mary Woolley after she was severely disabled by a stroke toward the end of her life. Mount Holyoke was Mary Woolley's home community and her extended family until a bitter struggle accompanied her departure and replacement in 1937. She never returned to the college campus after her retirement and died ten years later in 1947. This pattern of friendship was followed by many faculty.

Mount Holyoke was, in a manner of speaking, the "world turned upside down." In this college community special efforts were made to make men marginal. Men were the ones who were members of a minority and slow to advance in the faculty ranks; men were often even ignored when they tried to speak at faculty meetings. It was the mirror image of faculty gender relations elsewhere. Women not only ran the college and demonstrated strength and intellectual capabilities, but sustained each other in the nonwork setting as well.[16]

At the same time Mount Holyoke became a very intense and conflict-laden community. The parochial squabbles were substantively no different from those found in other small schools of whatever gender. But because the women lived and worked in an intense, competitive atmosphere without much occasion for involvement or emotional release elsewhere, personal animosities were perhaps more visible. Sometimes they plagued the departments.

During her tenure, Woolley never allowed such problems to have destructive consequences.[17] Never losing sight of her larger goals for women's professional advancement, she managed these tensions in a variety of ways. She always let it be known that her primary goal, and one that she put before community relations, was to facilitate intellectual work. Viola Barnes, who in the course of her long career at Mount Holyoke was involved in a variety of her own quarrels and disputes, described Woolley's success as a mediating influence in resolving a major conflict between Barnes and her superior, Nellie Neilson, head of the history department. After assuring Barnes of her continued employment, Woolley called her into the president's office and, in Barnes's words, reminded her:

> "Now you are in the lower rank there. I have given the department chairmen absolute control. If any row comes up in any department between a head and a member of that department, I have to stand by the head. That is a part of the system as I have introduced it. . . . So I am asking you, won't you please give in, whenever anything happens. . . . But . . . if it touches your work, either your teaching or your research, you stand by your guns and I'll stand by you." Now, wasn't that wonderful? [18]

As the college expanded, the president was very innovative in keeping peace among feuding factions. On several occasions she created an entirely new department primarily to accommodate a dissident faculty member whose continued contribution she particularly valued. This method was used, for instance, to separate political science and political economy from English. And Woolley's personal presence served to alleviate some of the worst fallout of these internecine quarrels.

Nevertheless, managing this special female community, which had few models in the larger society, was a major, unrelenting task. [19] Because the idea of a professional community for women was experimental and controversial, even relatively conventional squabbles could easily invite outside skeptics to criticize the whole enterprise. And because the college administrators were women, critics found additional opportunity to call female leadership into question.

Perhaps the greatest challenge to the reform and professionalization of the women's college was the continual need to assuage the worst fears of prospective students, parents, donors, and trustees, all of whom still harbored serious concerns about defying conventional definitions of femininity. The administration, supported by faculty leaders, did battle on many fronts and were often forced to reveal different faces to their varied constituencies.

Sounding the note that would echo as a refrain for more than three decades, Woolley outlined her approach in her inaugural address of 1901. She spoke first of her understanding of the changes in the value of higher education that had occurred during the 1890s. Education, she declared, was preparation for teaching on all levels, for social service, and for invention. The young, forward-looking president went on to exalt scholarship as an excellent pursuit for a young woman who has a "genius for detail, accuracy and perseverance wrought into her nature by generations of training in her home province." These feminine qualities "especially fit her for scientific and historical research, and her sense of proportion and application of the beautiful, aid her in her work of criticism." The president was quick to add, "nor is she incapable of the broad generalization, the wide outlook demanded by the scholar." Ever conscious of the struggle for equality in higher education, Woolley did not miss the opportunity to remind her audience that "the time seems not far distant when it will be conceded that the ability to master certain lines of thought is a question of the ability and not of sex."[20]

However high-minded these pronouncements may have sounded, they did not save Mary Woolley from the need to give lengthy explanations about her purposes and her willingness to comply with socially acceptable ideas. One donor, in a letter to the president, challenged the right of the religion department to employ critical analysis in teaching the Bible and made her displeasure very clear.

> I am writing you in regard to the chair in Biblical study I founded in your college, for one of the students whom I saw some time ago told me of what a trying experience she had had on account of her teacher being destructive in her criticism and sweeping away faith without putting any-thing in its place. . . . I am rather disappointed as you may imagine for my idea was to teach what the Bible says, rather than to go into the higher criticism and into what men say about the Bible.[21]

In her response Mary Woolley had to convince the donor of her commitment to the development of Christian piety in impressionable young women while not giving way on her greater commitment to rigorous standards of scholarship, including biblical criticism. In her reply Woolley first summarized the state of the department, explaining her dissatisfaction with the faculty who were holdovers from the previous administration, and reviewed her need to make temporary appointments until more qualified candidates could be found to build a department according to modern standards. The last paragraph of Woolley's lengthy reply indicates the variety of the sometimes contradictory demands she was forced to render coherent. Summarizing her goals, she replied

> In the first place, the permanent head of the department must have as thorough and fine an academic training as any member of the Faculty. The girls are very quick in making comparisons and they must be impressed with the fact that the instructing of the Bible demands as thorough preparation as the teaching of Biology or philosophy. Then she, (if it is a she!) must have the teacher's power of [illegible] and holding interest as well as of imparting knowledge.

Recognizing that she could not afford to alienate a wealthy donor, she concluded,

> Most important of all, there must be Christian character with all the moral earnestness and spiritual power which that should imply.[22]

Admittedly, the issue of religious instruction was apt to be a tricky one in any college in this period. What made Woolley's position particularly difficult was that questions of Christian morality were apt to be more heated at female institutions than at comparable male institutions. Any deviation from expected standards could be more easily blamed on the shortcomings of female instruction generally, rather than on specific individuals. At the same time, many donors and parents expected a girls' college to veer away from rigorous scholarship and move toward piety and character building. In short, in interaction with a disgruntled donor or parent, President Woolley had to allay the additional misgivings that women's institutions might generate. She had to be self-conscious about her attempt to develop a gender-free education in a culture that overwhelmingly adhered to the double sexual standard, in which women were believed to be morally superior, but socially and intellectually inferior.

The demand to yield to "appropriate education" for middle-class ladies was not confined to religious instruction. Woolley's administration was characterized by accommodation to certain conventional expectations, except when she believed it compromised the academic standards she was committed to developing and maintaining. Professor Ellen Deborah Ellis, first a member of the history department and later chair of the new political science department, recalled how unrelenting the struggle had been.

> A significant example of President Woolley's comprehension of the importance of protecting and pursuing the intellectual approach to an understanding of the facts of the universe . . . is revealed in her long and eventually successful struggle with a member of the Board of Trustees of Mount Holyoke in her resistance to his determination to allow courses in domestic science [home economics] toward the college degree. Through her persistence and that of her faculty, Mount Holyoke was thus saved from becoming a vocational school.[23]

Home economics was not introduced into the undergraduate curriculum; instead, Mount Holyoke students earned credits in chemistry or biology.[24]

Small women's colleges needed students now and jobs

for their graduates later, or at least potential prospects for employment. To ensure a sufficiently large student body, the president often sought to offer the public comforting and conventional impressions of what a woman's education might do for her. During and after World War I the demand for social service workers grew, and the colleges were quick to try to capitalize on these opportunities. "The outstanding fact of the war with regard to the colleges for women," Woolley told her board of trustees, "is that the value of the college to the common welfare was recognized as never before."[25] She cited the high praise of the Department of Economics and Sociology; these alumnae had contributed to the war effort, she explained, and physiologists were looking to the growing public health movement. If she could help it, she would allow no department to fall outside the new and compelling interest in social service: "The department of botany is emphasizing preparation for community service by . . . beginning the training of students to aiding fighting plant diseases with the hope that some students will be directed to take up the study of plant diseases as a profession."[26]

The main thrust of this postwar review to the board was to delineate acceptable routes for women graduates. Woolley argued that a liberal arts education could lead to a position in which knowledge was applied in a socially useful way. New fields, such as sociology or botany, provided expanding opportunities and were more receptive to women than were the older, more established fields. At the same time, these positions were socially acceptable and did not confront the power structure or challenge elite leadership positions held by men. Even when a graduate chose not to pursue a professional career, Mary Woolley suggested, while a wife and mother a woman could use her education to serve charitable causes.

Training women for original, creative, and autonomous work was not forgotten as a goal, but it was restricted to the professional development of the faculty and to a small group of student disciples whom the faculty would train as their successors. When the faculty turned to the business of selecting their disciples from the student body, the rhetoric of marriage and social acceptability waned and the struggle to attract the best minds took over. To ensure recruitment of the most talented, President Woolley urged the trustees to raise faculty salaries so the brightest of "young women as well as young men" would not be drawn off into more remunerative positions.[27] In the departments the values of the professional scholar prevailed; an examination of the Mount Holyoke history department illustrates what that meant to its members.

## THE NEW PROFESSIONAL FACULTY: SCHOLARLY MERIT AND THE RECRUITMENT OF PROGENY

In the second half of the nineteenth century, the Mount Holyoke history department was dominated by two long-standing faculty members, Elizabeth Prentiss and A. M. Soule. Prentiss, an 1862 graduate of Mount Holyoke Seminary, as it was then called, joined the faculty in

1864 and remained for forty years. The year she retired
(1904), the college conferred an M. A. on her in recognition of her abilities and long service. In the style of the
period, Elizabeth Prentiss "stressed history as a training
of the judgment." Her courses in modern history emphasized "the praise of ladies dead and lovely knights"
as a part of "the necessary equipment of an educated
woman."[28] Her students praised her for her humanity
and graciousness and for her wisdom as a teacher. She
had no conventional scholarly credentials—her only
publication appears to have been an outline of a Western
civilization course.[29]

Her colleague Miss Soule was younger and somewhat
more attuned to the introduction of new courses and
ideas. In what was then an innovation, she taught American history, and in that way anticipated the subsequent
introduction of political science and economics. She
even took her students on a field trip to observe factory
life in nearby, industrial Holyoke.[30] But like Prentiss she
engaged in no research and held no advanced degree.

Nellie Neilson and Bertha Putnam, who joined the
faculty in 1902 and 1908 respectively, stood in sharp contrast with their predecessors. The training and careers of
these two successors in the history department mark
a distinct break with past standards. Neilson and Putnam shared unconditional adherence to the new profes-

Opposite: Nellie Neilson. Courtesy of Mount Holyoke College Library/Archives.

sional ideas. They were superperformers in a separatist institution.

Neilson and Putnam shared many common interests and talents as well. Both were born in the early 1870s to affluent families, and both graduated in 1893 from Bryn Mawr, a new leader in women's education. Its president, M. Carey Thomas, was a significant advocate of rigorous scholarly training for women. She urged her students to consider academic careers, and both Neilson and Putnam fulfilled that vision.

Putnam and Neilson were highly influenced by Charles McLean Andrews, a well-known English institutional historian on the Bryn Mawr faculty. Nellie Neilson stayed on to work with him, and, after taking a leave to do research at Cambridge University in England, she received her doctorate from Bryn Mawr in 1899. After a few short teaching stints, she was appointed instructor in history at Mount Holyoke in 1902 and remained on the faculty until 1939, publishing many books and articles on the agrarian development of medieval England. Nellie Neilson received scholarly recognition and honors, from both English and American colleagues, of the kind that were rarely awarded to women historians.[31]

After receiving her B.A., Bertha Putnam left Bryn Mawr in 1893 to teach and assist her widowed father. She enrolled at Columbia University, earned a Ph.D. in 1908, and joined the Mount Holyoke faculty where she

Opposite: Bertha Putnam. Courtesy of Mount Holyoke College Library/Archives.

stayed until she retired in 1937. Like Nellie Neilson she was recognized for her scholarship in medieval English legal and economic history and was known as an excellent teacher. She received many honors and was awarded the first research grant ever given to a woman by Harvard Law School. Neither woman married. Although both traveled widely, they lived the rest of their lives in South Hadley, Massachusetts.[32]

Their deeply ingrained commitment to scholarship had implications for teaching as well as research. As one of her students subsequently observed, Nellie Neilson "would deny that she had any responsibility for moulding of character. Her concern was with the brains and not the morals of her students."[33] The shift to a professional model at Mount Holyoke entailed the adoption of new values about the meaning of work. The professional would not only hold special degrees, but also would specialize in a particular subfield of the discipline. She would not only do scholarly research, but also define herself as part of a larger professional group. To the extent that women were permitted, she would join the increasingly influential professional organizations, such as the American Historical Association and the Medieval Academy.[34]

Neilson, like most of her colleagues in this five-to-six-person history department, was self-conscious about her role as a female pioneer in the newly emerging world of modern scholarship. Committed to a full and active life as a researcher, she refused to allow the teaching obligations of a small college to absorb all of her energies. She ultimately gained widespread recognition from her colleagues at other institutions; for many years she was the only woman invited to join the Medieval Academy of America, and finally in 1943, at the very end of her career, she became a national figure with her election as the first woman president of the American Historical Association.[35]

Not surprisingly, the reputation of the Mount Holyoke department flourished under the leadership of Nellie Neilson and Bertha Putnam. In Putnam's obituary published in the *London Times* (1960), she was cited accurately as one of that "dwindling band of American historians who have contributed so greatly to our knowledge of English institutions in the Middle Ages."[36] English historians, who were ordinarily reluctant to accept either Americans or women into their ranks, acknowledged that "under her and her colleague Nellie Neilson Mount Holyoke became a notable focus of medieval, legal, and economic historical studies."[37]

The careers of these women became models for others in the department. Ellen Ellis, an early promoter of the study of international relations, and Viola Barnes, who taught American history, shared their highly professionalized goals and values, although they never achieved the same degree of fame. Ellis too was part of the prestigious Bryn Mawrter group at the college, a handful of Bryn Mawr graduates who became influential at Mount Holyoke and whose careers embodied a steadfast commitment to rigorous scholarship, frequent publication, and active engagement in professional associations.[38]

## EXPANDING THE NETWORK: THE DEVELOPMENT OF PROGENY

The history department, like many others at the college, took seriously the mandate of creating a new generation of scholars. Between 1899 and 1937, the college graduated almost nine hundred students who had majored in history. Neilson, Putnam, and their younger colleagues encouraged the best students to write honors papers and to go on to graduate school. Twenty-seven of these graduates (3.5 percent) subsequently earned the Ph.D., and 131 achieved at least a master's degree.[39] The creation of progeny was a significant enterprise that involved more than just sending promising students off to the major graduate schools: it depended on a set of beliefs about the importance of training the next generation to equal or surpass their mentors' own accomplishments. It also necessitated social and professional connections and opportunities that would enable faculty to assist young women to move into graduate training and help them in pursuing careers.

These opportunities were not readily available, and the faculty and administration persistently sought ways to create positions. The Mount Holyoke faculty was committed to expanding higher education for women nationally. They hoped that this, in turn, would create new opportunities for their professional progeny. A group of "daughter colleges" was planned that was to spread the Holyoke system well beyond the confines of South Hadley, Massachusetts.

Some graduates exercised continuing leadership in

PROFESSIONAL SCHOLARS IN ISOLATED SPLENDOR

administrative posts. In her 1908–1909 president's report, Mary Woolley proudly announced the appointment of a faculty member to the presidency of Lake Erie College, "one of Mount Holyoke's daughter colleges." She explained that "Not only does it mean that one of her alumnae, for several years a member of the faculty, takes the leadership of this daughter college in the Middle West, but also that what may be called the 'Mount Holyoke succession' of presidents of Lake Erie, remains unbroken."[40]

As the faculty anticipated, a large number of those who subsequently achieved the Ph.D. emulated their professors by entering academic life. Some taught at the daughter colleges, others went farther afield. Their success can be measured not only by the numbers of students who achieved advanced degrees, but also in the striking range and accomplishments of many of them. For example, two Mount Holyoke history graduates went on to build careers at a level of eminence that qualified them to be among the few female recipients of the prestigious Guggenheim fellowship. They were examples of a much larger group of productive, publishing scholars in the tradition of their undergraduate mentors.[41] For male scholars this sort of scholarly activity was more likely to be modeled on their professors at graduate school. The women's accomplishments become even more noteworthy when one considers that they did not have access to employment in research institutions but spent their entire professional careers in small teaching colleges.

This was the generation of women who entered Mount

Holyoke after World War I and professional life in the late 1920s or early 1930s. Their teachers pinned their hopes on these women for the future of women's professional employment. Their pioneering mentors were keenly aware of the obstacles that prevented even qualified women from participating fully in the larger academic world. They believed, however, that the special circumstances of the female enclave would serve as the seedbed of a small and continuous crop of gifted offspring, who would not only provide stimulation and regeneration for their faculty ranks but would also expand the small universe of female scholarship.

## THE IMPLICATIONS OF THE NEW SCHOLARSHIP FOR WOMEN

The educational reforms these pioneering academics sought depended on their notion that a great part of their energy had to be spent in demonstrating that women's intellectual capacities and potential for achievement were the equal of men's. Their efforts may now appear as a narrow construction of feminist goals. At the time, they represented a radical challenge to the status quo and to pervasive beliefs about women's inferiority. Because the women viewed the problem largely in rational terms and were firmly committed to notions of merit and achievement, they were convinced that the demonstration of female achievement would win great support and provide equal opportunities in the future.

In intellectual terms this meant that their profound commitment to merit and superperformance as teachers and scholars led them to develop ideas about research that were similar to those of male historians. They resisted adamantly any formulation of questions about gender as an appropriate category of analysis for an understanding of political and social institutions. They may have seen women's experience as distinctive. But they never translated this judgment into the more radical posture that might have required formulating a new set of intellectual questions that would have confronted the assumptions of the double standard.[42] The very impressive record of the Mount Holyoke history department is a case in point. It was no accident that the historiographical style adopted by the distinguished faculty members was in institutional and constitutional history, for that was the cutting edge of historical inquiry at the time and almost exclusively a male professional activity.

Even more significant, the focus of inquiry was also limited to male experience. The profound determination and enthusiasm of these women to excel in what were then new areas of scholarship was in no way diminished by the absence of women from this particular view of the past. In fact, these scholars viewed this focus on male endeavor as a desirable and justifiable rejection of the older sentimental, antiquarian traditions, which had delighted in what Nellie Neilson disparagingly called "the praise of ladies dead and lovely knights."[43] By contrast, historians using modern, objective methods of historical inquiry had defined institutional and political history as the prime focus of intellectually rigorous scholarship. Women historians' sense of appropriate postures of objectivity and the intellectual distance that proper inquiry was presumed to require insulated them from concern about omitting the areas of historical inquiry in which women might have been included.

It is in light of their rejection of an older and "softer" tradition of style and inquiry that we can better understand their unreserved devotion to the intellectual leadership of such giants in the field as F. W. Maitland or William Stubbs. Although their allegiance was certainly explicable in strictly intellectual terms (political and institutional questions were the exciting historical foci of the period), Neilson and Putnam also saw no problem with prospective young female scholars devoting themselves to a mode of inquiry and a subject matter almost exclusively preoccupied with England's male ruling class. In fact, there was an attractive refinement in the majestic sweep of their dispassionate inquiries into constitutional questions and ruling elites. If gender was considered at all, it must have seemed beside the point—or a rude intrusion of something the female scholars were determined to forget in their work. What Neilson and her colleagues emphasized was the importance of the intellectual challenge and the requirement of rigor in work that transcended the personal predispositions of the historian. In her often-repeated quote from the constitutional historian William Stubbs, Neilson expressed a whole generation's view of the arduous nature of scholarship:

> The history of Institutions cannot be mastered, can scarcely be approached without an effort. It affords little of the romantic incident or of the picturesque grouping which constitute the charm of History in general, and holds out

small temptation to the mind that requires to be tempted to the study of Truth.

This was not only a study that precluded "charm" and "the romantic," but constitutional history in particular also warranted special praise because, Stubbs continued,

> Without some knowledge of Constitutional History it is absolutely impossible . . . to understand the origin of parties, the development of principles, the growth of nations in spite of parties and in defiance of principles. It alone can teach why it is that in politics good men do not always think alike, that the worst cause has often been illustrated with the most heroic virtue, and that the world owes some of its greatest debts to men from whose very memory it recoils.[44]

These were the truly significant questions with which the scholar had to be concerned if she wished to be taken seriously. For women scholars the need to document their seriousness was especially acute. Not surprisingly, no critique of this kind of study would be forthcoming from them. They were required, in the nature of the case, to offer the fiercest and most unquestioning commitment in order to compensate for any lingering doubts evoked by their gender.[45] In these circumstances, it was unlikely that even the most talented women historians would attempt to formulate questions that included female experience as a paramount focus.

Their excitement about being on the cutting edge of English constitutional and economic history affected students for two decades. In the following generation, however, the founders' initial success in creating excellent students who would be the next group of committed scholars was not to be repeated. Thereafter, it became more difficult to find students who would choose to follow this increasingly arduous path. In part, this decline was due to the larger social and economic circumstances of the Great Depression and the concomitant competition for scarce employment.

Economic austerity put additional financial pressure on the small colleges, squashing any hope the visionary leaders may have had for expanded control of graduate education for women. Mount Holyoke's small master's program remained just that, never expanding to award the most esteemed professional degree, the doctorate, a significant goal that some presidents of women's colleges had called for as early as 1908.[46]

The fact that doctoral programs failed to develop from the fledgling master's offerings ultimately consigned the women's colleges to a subordinate status in the professional hierarchy. By the 1930s the hegemony of the research universities was fully in place. To the extent that employment at undergraduate institutions did not expand in ways that they had anticipated, women's opportunities contracted rather than expanded, for there were to be few opportunities for them at coeducational institutions. Unlike their counterparts in the single-sex male colleges, neither graduates nor ambitious mobile faculty from Mount Holyoke, Wellesley, and other comparable women's schools could easily rely on access to research-oriented graduate departments.[47] Even the best women faculty from Mount Holyoke, Smith, or Wellesley did not receive offers from the University of Wisconsin, Yale, or the University of California. This lack of access narrowed their possibilities for producing future scholarly progeny. Similarly, the graduates of these colleges had fewer opportunities for admission to prestigious graduate departments than did graduates of Amherst, Williams, or Wesleyan.

The pioneers' mission was even more diluted in the small daughter colleges, further removed from the fountainhead of inspiration as they were and struggling to accommodate the prosaic needs of middle-class girls, whose postgraduate goals seldom went beyond marriage and family life. The small daughter colleges did not recruit the pioneering students who came, albeit in limited numbers, to the increasingly elite "Seven Sisters." This erosion of a student constituency prepared to emulate its teachers had serious consequences for the viability and strength of separatist institutions in cultivating opportunities for graduates and in gaining leverage on a role in national academic leadership.

## THE QUESTION OF MARRIAGE AND THE LIMITS OF SEPARATISM

Diminishing professional opportunities were often complicated by the continual reemergence of the marriage question. Like Mary Woolley, Nellie Neilson and Bertha Putnam understood that by emphasizing the need to achieve intellectual equality and create a new generation of professionals they were at odds with the ideals and practices of conventional family life, but their solutions never went beyond personal and individual rejection of marriage. To the extent that they fought against conventional expectations regarding marriage, it was a silent war. Only occasional comments revealed their heightened sensitivity to the damage that marriage could do to their professional aspirations. "Weddings have wrought havoc in the ranks of the faculty and staff," President Woolley told her board of trustees in her 1923 report. Many were "resigning or refusing reappointment at the close of the last academic year for that reason."[48] Marriage, it was understood, presented an either/or choice: one could not have a husband and a career.

At the beginning of the century, women scholars at Mount Holyoke seem to have had an abiding faith that the intellectual life, as experienced at a small women's college, would be sufficiently attractive to recruit a regular supply of outstanding students. In the initial years, when the president of Mount Holyoke reassured parents and trustees that their offerings enhanced a woman's capacity to be wife and mother, she was entirely sincere. But she always said it with the implicit confidence that the truly committed minority would forego marriage and opt for the special joys of professional life. For some women the single life was clearly preferable to marriage; for the majority who did marry, the conflict between marriage and career foreshortened their professional possibilities.[49]

It is easier in hindsight to see the problems of precluding married women than it must have been for scholars in the first flush of excitement of women's entrance into higher education. The fact remains that the leaders, among both faculty and administration, did not reexamine the problematic dynamic between professional life and marriage and, by extension, the relationship between men and women. Even though the marriage rate among college graduates was increasing in the first two decades of the twentieth century, these professionals resisted that trend. They assumed that to be a wife meant that one had to be a subordinate and that this inevitably contaminated professional aspirations and achievement. Therefore, marriage had to be rejected by serious professionals.[50]

These views were continually reinforced by the men whom they met socially, by the policies of the colleges in which they worked, and even, at times, by other women. One outspoken, albeit anonymous, professor at another institution expressed her own resentments against this either/or choice: "I have not found that ready masculine comprehension which I could have wished of my own deep-seated, and as I think legitimate, feeling that it would be an unspeakable sacrifice to exchange the work to which my best efforts and dearest ambitions have been given for a life of pure domesticity merely for the considerably overestimated boon of being supported, no matter how well."[51] She goes on to delineate some of the unacceptable response she had received from men: "The male attitude of mind I have found to vary from a mild objection about my ideas of professional life for married women as "impracticable" to a fierce jealousy which refuses to tolerate the suggestion that a woman may possibly love at once her profession and her husband."[52]

The faculty at Mount Holyoke optimistically believed

that they had found in the separatist enclave a socially acceptable solution to the problem that had traditionally plagued women's aspirations; at least separatism seems to have enabled them to avoid confronting publicly the common assumptions regarding the paramount importance of the domestic role for women. Earlier, the women's colleges had proven, through their own example, that intellectual life need not be physically debilitating to women, when the conventional wisdom and the medical profession insisted otherwise. Now the colleges wanted to create a setting to prove that professional women could live challenging lives dedicated to intellectual pursuits and that the ideal of marriage and children was not so much an issue to be rejected as a model that was irrelevant.

They sought their solution in the single life; personally compelling for this group of pioneers as such a life was, it would prove more problematic for future generations. Their rejection of matrimony was radical in the short run and not entirely effective in the long run. By casting the question in either/or terms, marriage or career, they precluded a risky search for new directions for women in marriage and in the professions and offered a narrower spectrum of options. Ultimately, their sense of mission was an inadequate defense against the overwhelming pressure for subsequent generations to opt for matrimony.

By the 1930s, even women most committed to the life of the single scholar recognized that marriage was the rock on which the whole dream might founder. At this point, even the most promising students were being attracted to married life. The "woman question" was changing from an earlier formulation—could women physiologically and intellectually embrace higher learning—to a modern version: could women combine marriage and professional life? The same faculty women who had earlier urged promising scholars to sacrifice the conventional roles of wife and mother now exhorted young married women not to abandon entirely their professional aspirations.

Speaking to alumnae in 1939, Nellie Neilson reflected this shift in position when she entreated her audience to continue "their studies after matrimony, in spite of the many problems involved." Her own goals remained sufficiently unchanged to warrant her adding that "This is a matter in which I am much interested for the advancement of productive scholarship." And she bravely continued with the worried admonition, "Do not give up the ship necessarily and forever when you marry. Do not just help your husband in another field than your own."[53]

In few instances is the reversal on the relation between marriage and profession more clearly documented than in the case of President M. Carey Thomas, who once spoke out so forcefully on the need for women to develop serious professional careers and who had led Bryn Mawr to create a powerful center of scholarship and graduate education. The reversal, it must be added, focused on others and not herself; for her, scholarship and education always remained the paramount goal. Even as a young, nineteenth-century woman embarking on graduate study in Germany with her friend Mamie Gwynn, she had found a clear sense of purpose and satisfaction in the thought that "most women's lives were spent in clearing things out of one place to put them in another, and that we had forsaken that sphere."[54] Her sense of dissatisfaction with women's traditional role went beyond disenchantment with domestic responsibilities to include a rejection of child rearing: "If a woman has children I do not see but what she will have to at least for some time, give up her work, and of all things, taking care of children does seem the most utterly unintellectual."[55] At the end of her life, Thomas looked on her favorite niece's marriage as an apostasy.

Nonetheless, in her later years Thomas was not without hope that the seemingly ineluctable decision to marry could yet be accommodated to the "Cause." Rather than sending her niece, Millicent Carey McIntosh, the expected conventional letter of congratulations, Thomas put down her ideas about marriage, a condition that she believed should be molded to fit her most ardent yearnings for increasing the public role of women. "On the pro side of the question," she wrote,

> We have the possibility that you and he will be able to make a "genuine contribution" as the social workers say, to the all important burning question of whether a married woman can hold down a job as successfully as an unmarried woman. This must be proved over and over again before the woman question can get much further and I have set my heart on your making a success of it and so bringing great help to the "Cause."[56]

She went on with several pages of advice to the young bride, comprised of an uneasy mixture of the rather

modern insistence on the need to maintain one's autonomy within marriage mixed with admonitions about
the consequences of physical intimacy between husband
and wife. On this point she cautioned her niece that

> If I were starting out as you are to make the greatest pos-
> sible success of a husband and a job I should take every le-
> gitimate means to preserve his illusion about me. I should
> never occupy one room with him. . . . Make it a fixed rule
> on the steamer, in all hotels that you are firm. . . . Do not
> stay with people who will not or cannot give you two
> rooms. Stay in an hotel and eat your meals with them.[57]

Whatever else one may make of this advice to the bride,
it is clear that Thomas perceived the marital state as an
enveloping menace for the professional wife. Still, one
may detect that she was relenting, at least to acknowledge some need to accommodate to the presence of a
husband. She knew that this generation, unlike the successful women of her time, would not reject marriage
entirely.

Ultimately, this shift in posture to a more favorable
view of the "marriage question" became the only available response in light of the declining appeal of the
single life. But even this proved to be too little too late
for the continuous recruitment of progeny. In their three
decades of control of the women's colleges, feminists had
certainly proven that women were capable of scholarly
endeavor. What they had not done was to examine the
marriage question, nor, even more to the point, had
they generated new models of faculty and administrative
careers that included substantial numbers of married
women.[58] Mount Holyoke had had no married women

on its permanent faculty. Ironically, this lack of role models threatened the scholars' ability to create successors within a new generation of recruits imbued with equal dedication to scholarship and to academic separatism, if not to the single life.

## THE DECLINE OF THE SEPARATIST IDEAL

The resurgence of customary marriage expectations overwhelmed the countervailing, and increasingly exceptional, models represented by the unmarried faculty couples of the women's colleges. The fight over the succession to the presidency, when Mary Woolley retired in 1937, symbolized the end of an era of female leadership and feminist ideology at Mount Holyoke, the most zealous of women's colleges. Mary Woolley's replacement by an unremarkable, male associate professor from Yale represented the victorious incursion of conservative forces with conventional notions of womanhood. It was a shift that could no longer be controlled. For years the feminist leaders had offered flaccid assurances to trustees, parents, and donors that Mount Holyoke would train prospective wives and mothers. The demand for a conventional feminine setting ultimately overtook the separatist ethos that held commitment to scholarly excellence as its highest goal.[59] This did not happen, however, without a struggle that polarized the community. The appointment of Roswell Gray Ham as president was the harbinger of a new style of leadership. The president's house would now be occupied by a married man, whose wife would function as a gracious hostess and whose children further attested to the joys of family life.[60]

The development of separatism as a strategy for women, and its demise, went well beyond the women's colleges. As Estelle Freedman among others has shown, the late nineteenth century saw the flowering of the women's clubs, the suffrage movement, the settlement houses, and a variety of other separate women's organizations. These institutions offered women opportunities to articulate and defend their own interests and build female networks; they offered leadership opportunities to the most committed and talented.[61] In the 1920s when the "new" woman sought opportunities in male institutions and thought that the newly acquired right to vote would ensure her integration into political life, separatism declined.

The strategies and goals adopted by the academics at Mount Holyoke clearly were inspired by a range of needs and possibilities. The female faculty were well aware of the circumstances of other women's organizations. They were in touch with professional colleagues throughout the country. Yet their experience had some distinctive qualities. Even at the height of their separatism the female academics generally accepted male standards for their scholarship, for curriculum development, and for professional recognition. They rarely saw themselves as persons who could bring special female qualtities of nurturance or morality to the world of scholarship. They did not want to make public the concerns of the private sphere, such as health or child rearing, as did women in the temperance movement, who were concerned, at least initially, with preserving the morality of the family. Nor did they develop a radical opposition to male standards of professionalism. Woolley, Neilson, Putnam, and their colleagues hoped to redefine the private sphere, bending its parameters so that it would support an enriched, but separate, professional life for women.

Faculty and administration alike knew that small colleges were competing against increasingly well-equipped and amply funded universities where research was becoming highly specialized. The uneven conditions continued to plague them as they had to teach more classes, attend more committee meetings, and struggle for research time and money. As Virginia Drachman has shown in her study of the New England Hospital for Women, separatism in medicine declined when women physicians began to think that they could be trained in more modern hospitals.[62]

As separatism declined elsewhere, two situations remained the same at Mount Holyoke. First, the college remained committed to providing excellent undergraduate education for women only. This goal was possible and desirable because it meant that the college did not have to stretch scarce resources for graduate training as New England Hospital and others attempting to offer advanced training had done. Second, Neilson's and Putnam's students had largely gone on to coeducational university graduate schools, and this continued even though they faced discrimination and quota systems. But finding jobs for the most highly qualified graduates proved increasingly difficult; also, women more and more resisted opting for careers over marriage.

PROFESSIONAL SCHOLARS IN ISOLATED SPLENDOR

The post–World War II shift in policy that encouraged the appointment of male faculty in women's colleges was the coup de grace. In the conservative postwar period, the appointment of significant numbers of men to the faculties of the women's colleges was supposed to signal a commitment to the highest professional standards. It meant hiring Ph.D.s from Harvard, Yale, Princeton, and Columbia, the most prestigious training grounds for male academics. In the competition for jobs, women found that single-sex women's colleges were no longer as receptive to having predominantly female faculties. Women faculty, who still tended to be excluded from tenure track positions at most male and coeducational institutions, now began losing ground in the former female preserves.[63]

It is a tribute to the outstanding accomplishments of the early educational leaders that this retreat from their original vision did not signal the demise of these important institutions. The women's colleges, as respected providers of female undergraduate education, were to serve as the locus for a new wave of feminism that would profit by the colleges' mistakes as well as by their contributions. If modern feminists have a heightened sense of the relationship between the values of the wider society and those of academe, if they are more concerned about reexamining the conditions of women in marriage and the relationship between the sexes, and if they define their intellectual goals more widely to include women's experience, they come to these enlarged visions through the experience and achievements of the feminist scholars at the turn of the century.

# MOTHERHOOD AND MEDICINE

Although a substantial minority of women practiced medicine in the latter part of the nineteenth century, only a few women were admitted to the new, laboratory-based medical schools at the turn of the century.[1] Like most aspiring professionals, they were apt to be women of extraordinary drive and achievement. Their professional ambitions were strong enough to withstand the rigid norms of a society that assumed women should marry and stay at home. They had to compete first for admission to medical school and later for coveted internships and hospital staff positions in a profession that actively sought to eliminate them from its ranks. An examination of women's entrance into the medical profession at the end of the nineteenth century and in the early decades of the twentieth offers an opportunity to analyze the experience of women in a profession that was male dominated, attempting to control membership, and increasingly inhospitable to the aspirations of outsiders.

To succeed in this field where male candidates were favored (at the same time that standards of meritocracy were touted), many women chose the strategy of superperformance. There was as well a separatist alternative: some women attended the women's medical schools. But these graduates, once trained, still had to compete with men for professional places and relied on extraordinary achievements to obtain the ordinary professional rewards.[2]

Since as successful physicians they were supposed to

dedicate long hours and extraordinary energy to their professional life, marriage represented a special problem for these women. Male colleagues could choose whether or not to marry. Bachelor or husband, either choice was acceptable, though the decision to marry normally enhanced men's professional possibilities. The reverse was true for women. Women who chose to remain single were considered deviant; furthermore, they lacked the assistance that men could expect from a spouse. Nevertheless, singlehood was still the preferred path; in the early period of modern medicine most female physicians did not marry.

The position of token woman—the isolated individual functioning with, but never fully accepted by, the male enclave—was very difficult. On the one hand, it offered some possibilities for ambitious and talented individuals. At the same time it evoked uncertainty and doubt about their proper role, both as physicians and as women. This ambiguity had a serious impact on marriage decisions. Most chose not to combine the two separate and contradictory sets of demands that came from work and family. Well-known physicians such as Florence Sabin, Alice Hamilton, and S. J. Baker remained single and devoted themselves almost entirely to their careers.

The minority who did marry faced a serious problem

Opposite: Dorothy Reed Mendenhall, 1919, Washington, D.C. Mendenhall Collection. Courtesy of Sophia Smith Collection, Women's History Archive, Smith College.

in the unavoidable disjuncture between the different expectations society had for their public and private lives. Married women often found that superperformance was not nearly as effective a strategy after marriage as it had been before. Although the number of married women physicians was still relatively low, it increased with every decade. We will focus on two of these extraordinary pioneers because they illustrate the professional choices available to aspiring women physicians, the particular strategies they used, and the impact of marriage on their careers.

Dorothy Reed's (Mendenhall) early career pattern met the highest male standards of medical training and practice. Although she encountered many obstacles along the way, she overcame them with the determination and extraordinary ability characteristic of the superperformer. She was one of the rare few who received a fine undergraduate education as well as the best medical training and postgraduate internship. Her early career augured colleagueship with the most prestigious doctors in the finest hospitals.

Marriage, for Reed, was the single event that shifted this career path. Difficult as the path to high professional status was for single women, it was further complicated by the decsion to marry. Although Reed was to resume professional work after marriage, her career trajectory would never be the same. To accommodate her private

Opposite: Anne Walter Fearn on graduation from Women's Medical College. From 1939 autobiography.

life, she had to devise new and creative positions in her public life that were outside the conventional professional routes. She would no longer travel with the elite establishment at the forefront of medicine. By virtue of her decision to marry and have children, she was relegated to the periphery of the medical profession.[3]

Anne Walter Fearn followed the more typical nineteenth-century path to medical school. She did not attend a liberal arts college. She enrolled in the Women's Medical College of Pennsylvania, an institution that had been established by women for female students who were usually denied access to men's schools.[4] Unlike Reed, virtually all of Fearn's professional career was spent in China: here she provided medical services to persons who would otherwise have had no access to Western medical care.

While she remained single, Fearn was free to stay in China or to return to the United States. Her marriage to a missionary determined that her career would permanently unfold in China, a setting far removed from conventional professional life and its strictures. Both Reed's and Fearn's lives illustrate the special structural limitations placed on even the most ambitious and talented married women during a period noteworthy for the expanding opportunities it offered men of their class and background.

Both women struggled with the problems of being female, and especially of being wives. They both married relatively late, after considerable thought, yet still had some reservations about combining profession and marriage.[5] They struggled to create a satisfactory family life that did not stifle their professional ambitions. Although they were devoted to their husbands and children, domesticity proved quite disagreeable and even painful at times. They never became fully enmeshed in the "appropriate" activities of ordinary, middle-class wives—charity, church, and clubs. Work was their most satisfying and demanding outlet, yet it filled them with unrelenting conflicts.

Each chose a different style of career management to cope with her own, and society's, attitudes toward women physicians who chose to marry. For Reed, the greatest barriers to professional success were to occur after she had successfully obtained her M.D. from the most prestigious school of the time. For Fearn the postgraduate problem of where to practice and choice of clientele was resolved when she moved to a foreign country where there was virtually no competition from men trained in Western methods. By American standards neither physician ever earned a high income from her medical practice. Before examining the lives of these two women, it is useful to discuss the changes that the medical profession was undergoing and the impact of those changes on women.

## KEEPING WOMEN OUT

Prejudices against women's equal participation showed up in various ways as medical opportunities evolved. As medicine was modernized, the rewards of participation and the concern with exclusivity increased. As new standards and expectations of professional endeavor were defined, opportunities also arose, both formal and informal, for denying entrance to those who did not qualify or, if qualified academically, failed to fit the desired mold because of race, ethnicity, class, or gender. For physicians professional success came to depend increasingly on being admitted to a modern, well-funded, and well-equipped medical school. Moreover, graduates needed to acquire internships in a high-ranking specialty, representation on newly empowered licensing boards, staff positions in reputable hospitals, promotions in the ranks of expanding medical faculties, and leadership positions, or at least a voice, in the increasingly powerful professional associations.[6]

But these opportunities were hedged about with biases and restrictions against lower classes, against minority ethnic groups, and certainly against women. Many of these requirements for success were only barely emerging in the late nineteenth and early twentieth centuries, but this lack of a long tradition of expectation made them no less significant in the gathering momentum for professional expansion and status. Reed and Fearn, like other women physicians, were of the "right" class, color, and educational background. Only their gender marred their acceptability.

Preference on the basis of sex, class, race, or ethnicity was nothing new and hardly confined to new professions. What made the women's case particularly complex was the mixed message sent by the medical establishment. It boasted about meritocracy and emphasized that access was granted on the basis of individual ability. The profession's main claim to superiority over rival healing and training programs, moreover, was based on its allegiance to objectivity and science.[7] The very stuff of medical progress, with its heavy emphasis on scientific research, should have reinforced the ideal that earned so much lip service, the ideal of building a professional group on the basis of ability or merit alone. But the reality was different. In order to reconcile a meritocratic standard with the ill-concealed discrimination against certain groups, the medical schools, hospitals, and individual physicians had to construct arbitrary and often contradictory systems to determine who was admitted and who was not. In the process, they frequently held out false hopes to aspiring and qualified newcomers.

The arbiters of professional ideology argued that women could rarely become true professionals because their emotional temperament and training were unsuited to "dispassionate inquiry," increasingly touted as the central component of medical training. Women, they presumed, did not have the innate capacity for objectivity and detachment physicians needed to manage the myriad of emotional and intellectual problems they faced. They reasoned, moreover, that only this special capacity to use the scientific method legitimized deep probing into the nature of life and death. The higher goal of scientific inquiry, for instance, permitted physicians to violate their patients' personal modesty. In the healing relationship, in addition, a patient could be expected to reveal not only physical problems, but also emotional and even moral concerns. For this level of intimacy, it was argued, women were clearly not suited.[8]

The irony is apparent. Given medicine's interest in enlarging its role as an authority in moral and emotional problems, the new educational leaders might have argued (if there had been less prejudice against "the sex") that women's natural reproductive capacities, which put them directly in touch with natural functions, could actually enhance women's aptitude for this new style of healing. An earlier tradition of midwives, healers, and female doctors tied women to the natural world. The scientific, laboratory-based medical school could have incorporated those older values. Instead, the possibility that women might have natural predispositions to be healers came under attack. In the late nineteenth century, male practitioners, in the name of science, proclaimed that women lacked the higher order of intellect and reason required for scientific investigation and a commitment to rationality.[9] Their mental inferiority would keep them from making the logical leap, from the identification of microorganisms on the slide to the analysis of disease (of which there was very little reliable understanding by anyone).

Social barriers also kept women from the newly developed precincts of laboratory training. Presumably, the fragile female constitution, with its delicate sensibilities, could not be exposed to the horrors of the death house and the morgue. The myth of female sensitivity was strong enough to support a deep conviction that young women could not abide the stench or the suggestiveness of the nude cadaver. This belief hurt women in medical school: familiarity with a cadaver was essential in medical training. Furthermore, to combine such morbid activity with prospective motherhood was unthinkable. Given these values and perceptions, it was not difficult for the emerging medical establishment to create settings that virtually precluded women's participation. And these professional structures fit well with the larger drive toward exclusivity. By the turn of the century, the approved medical membership was overwhelmingly white, native born, middle class, and male.

## THE TOKEN FEW

In spite of these views, and the exclusive organizational mechanisms designed to bar women from the competition, some of them set out to join the ranks of the modern, scientifically trained physicians. Other more traditional colleagues received training in homeopathic institutions or in schools that taught other rival healing systems. In attempting to qualify as legitimate practitioners of medicine, an increasingly prestigious and elite group, women who succeeded in studying in the new, scientific medical schools were a special group. They were daring and ambitious, but their ambition evoked mixed feelings in others. As a result these unusual women also experienced feelings of ambivalence about themselves and their choices.

DOROTHY REED'S UNPUBLISHED MEMOIRS, A THOUSAND pages of recollections, were set down over a period of almost a decade and a half (1939–1953) near the end of her life. They reveal the private experience of a woman of Faustian ambition who tried to be both a dedicated physician and a devoted mother. With characteristic frankness and insight she tells us that there will be some omissions and unexplained passages "for I am a woman and Victorian but I shall write for my great granddaughter of the way my world was made, and what happened to me in the making and unmaking of it."[10] Her memoirs provide an unusually unsentimental, poignant, and literate record that points up the private satisfactions and stresses, as well as the public accomplishments, of this extraordinary woman. And they allow us to compare certain critical themes in her life with those of Anne Walter Fearn's and of others of their generation. We focus especially on the way in which her professional development was inextricably bound up with her maturation as a woman. She was ideologically committed to the idea that excellent performance would ultimately overcome any lingering prejudice against female participation. Yet in the end she had to come to terms with circumstances that forced unusual choices on her.

Reed's memoirs begin with the description of a childhood in an upper-middle-class family of conventional Victorian sensibilities. Although her father died when she was quite young, there was enough money for Dorothy to be educated in Europe by private tutors, as befitted young ladies of her class. We hear very little encouragement for breaking away from social conventions from her mother or other family members and see little in her background that points to her future career choice and life-style. Years later when she undertook to study medicine, it was still considered a highly questionable occupational choice for women. The medical training of the period meant that she had to violate Victorian standards of female modesty regarding bodily functions. Even the men of the period examined these "mysteries" rather self-consciously, and familiarity with such matters was considered unacceptable for women. These attitudes were manifested in various ways. For example, Henry M. Hurd, superintendent of Johns Hopkins Hospital and a physician of considerable influence at this most advanced institution, accused Reed of being a "sex pervert" when the new intern expressed a willingness to work in the male wards.[11]

Reed's own family apparently shared Hurd's evident repulsion toward her behavior. Only a few years earlier Dorothy's elder sister had accompanied her to Smith College for her freshman year. The sister wrote home to their mother with considerable discomfort that "it was no place for a well-brought up girl to stay" because, according to Dorothy, her sister "disapproved of the girls crowding the streets, calling out joyously to one another, hatless, and acting with freedom and abandon" which the well-protected Dorothy "had never seen before."[12]

Dorothy Reed graduated in 1895 from Smith college, one of the first institutions designed to offer women undergraduate training equal to that of the elite men's colleges and universities. She benefited, too, from the work of M. Carey Thomas and the Women's Committee of Baltimore, an older generation of determined feminists whose influence and money forced the reluctant but financially pressed founders of Johns Hopkins Medical

School to open their doors to women. Reed entered Johns Hopkins in 1896. Three years before the institution had begun its pioneering effort in modern medical education with a curriculum modeled primarily on the German medical schools.[13] Through the hard work of an earlier group of feminists, Reed and a small number of able and privileged young women could avail themselves of the best medical education in the United States. Reed's career was made possible by this access to modern education, with its concentration on laboratory methods and scientific research, and an enriched curriculum to convey the new discoveries in bacteriology. She went on to incorporate that learning into her professional life and achievements.

Reed wrote that it required "nearly ten years to accustom my mother to my being a doctor, which she had bitterly opposed."[14] And it was a measure of the "impropriety" of medical practice for women that her aunt claimed that Dorothy's example contributed to the delinquency of her younger female cousin. Reed resented the fact that relatives believed that she was "loose moraled like all women doctors."[15]

Of course, like most women trained at the end of the century, Reed had to prove herself repeatedly against the prejudices about female frailty. A generation had passed since 1878, when the Association for the Advancement of Medical Education of Women had found it necessary to defend the then daring proposition that women physicians would work in the infirmary as "faithfully, steadily, and perseveringly, as it could have been done by men," further that "it is very rare that the health of any of these [females] physicians fails under the work."[16] Nevertheless, Reed felt it necessary to do ward duty at Johns Hopkins for twelve months, rather than the usual ten that her male colleagues thought sufficient. In the suffocating heat of a Baltimore summer when the male interns had sensibly left for cooler climates and a brief rest, she was spurred to remain on the wards because of "something Dr. Hurd [the hospital superintendent] had said of woman's being irresponsible and not to be trusted to see things through."[17]

In her own eyes, Reed was not a trailblazer and preferred to minimize the differences between herself and her colleagues. Nevertheless, she was caught up in the pioneer's inevitable obligation to perform heroically. Numerous accounts by other women physicians corroborate this determination to prove that women were as able as men by doing more than was ordinarily expected.[18] And in these efforts it was always the male-defined standard that women believed they must match or exceed.

The twelve women in Reed's class comprised almost one-fourth of the group. Even so she knew that perceptions about women were mixed. In the first class at Johns Hopkins there had been three women. One married a professor and dropped out, one left to become a Christian Scientist, and one graduated with honors. Although there was greater academic success in the second and third classes, other criticisms arose.

Several women were in the class above me, the third class to enter, Blanche Etting and a frump named Delia Wyckill, who represented all that is undesirable in professional woman. She [Wyckill] was a good student and became an interne. The men always made fun of her, and told with glee how she took a day off every month to stay in bed when she menstruated leaving them to do the work. Hearing ribald tales my fourth year when I was on the wards, of her failings, I determined at least to ask no favor because of being a woman.[19]

Another contemporary, Emily Dunning Barringer, recounts at length the extraordinary efforts that were required of her during her internship as the first woman ambulance surgeon in New York. On her very first day she was deliberately assigned duty "for the routine catheterizations in the male surgical ward." This redoubtable pioneer recalled that "I could not quite believe my ears" and in stunned silence thought "There must be some mistake. Could it be possible that the first night they would assign me to this duty on the male ward? I felt as if a stick of dynamite with a burning sputtering fuse had been placed in my hands." This procedure had never been assigned to women since it was "one of the most intimate of all medical ministrations."[20]

Barringer's alarm was understandable, but this attempt to prove her unworthy fit a larger pattern of discrimination. The hospital administration had been loathe to admit her and made no provision for her personal needs, in part to signal its reluctance to accept a woman on the staff. In order to bathe she had to haul a portable bathtub into her room.[21] She had to have a special uniform made that would afford her official identity on ambulance calls. She was consistently given the hardest rotations in the hospital; she was called away during mealtimes to treat the maggot-infected ulcers of a patient. Missed meals were a special hardship because she could not, like her male colleagues, frequent the local saloon for an after-hours snack.[22]

For such women no task was too arduous, no personal risk too high or frightening, no patient too threatening, contagious, or vile. Superperformance can be understood partly as a counterphobic attempt by these pathbreakers to offer evidence opposed to long and deeply held beliefs about the image of the female—a weak and neuresthenic fragile flower.[23] Their extraordinary efforts also derived from their profound belief that meritorious performance would ultimately be recognized and rewarded.

Dorothy Reed, like her contemporaries, based her sense of achievement and professional attainments on male models of activity. She believed that one's work had the highest priority over one's personal life. She considered her femininity an intrusion that weakened the possibility of being taken as an expert of some substance. Toward this end she, like many women professionals, wished to make her physical differences as unnoticeable as possible.

Women physicians rose to the challenge of trying to be like men in every area of life. Very often they found seemingly irrelevant details to be major obstacles in asserting their equality. Their excessive concern with dress was a manifestation of the unspoken set of assumptions about women's need to be accepted as equals. Dr. S.

## MOTHERHOOD AND MEDICINE

Josephine Baker, an eminent contemporary of these women, describes the lengths to which she went so that her feminine appearance would not prove a distraction.

The Gibson Girl [style of clothing] was a great help to me when I started work in the public health field: It is difficult to realize today how curious it seems then [first decade of the twentieth century] that a woman should hold my position. [When she was made assistant to the commissioner of health] they made me print my name on the letterheads as "Dr. S. J. Baker" to disguise the presence of a woman in a responsible executive post. The Gibson Girl played a part in the situation because shirtwaists and tailored suits [became] a conventional feminine costume . . . if I was to be the only woman executive in the New York City department of Health, I badly needed protective coloring. . . . I could so dress that, when a masculine colleague of mine looked around the office in a rather critical state of mind, no feminine furbelows would catch his eye and give him an excuse to become irritated by the presence of a woman where, according to him, no woman had a right to be.

She appreciated the convenience of tailored clothing because it required little time or energy to care for:

in the process of convincing myself that my work must be a success and equal to the best that might be done by a man in that man-made world, I invariably took home a brief case full of trouble every night and worked at it until the small hours of the morning. Dr. Mary Walker wore trousers to startle men into recognizing that a woman was demanding man's rights. I wore a standard costume—almost a uniform—because the last thing I wanted was to be conspicuously feminine when working with men. [24]

Similarly, Barringer takes up the better part of a chapter in her memoirs with details about the challenge of dressing and notes that "perhaps no outfit of clothes was ever more carefully thought out, or agonized over, than that wardrobe of mine." [25]

Women felt they had to adopt the male values that judged femininity a distraction to professional work. This tended to engender considerable ambivalence in women, and the decision to marry often served to exacerbate their guilt and doubts rather than to resolve them. While those who remained single might sidestep some of the issues, those who were married were forced to face all the problems of being a woman. But even women who chose not to marry had to be careful not to lean too far in the other direction and call attention to themselves by being too mannish. They had to attempt the impossible task of not being enough of either sex to be noticed. They were afraid that any attention to their sexuality would result in the speedy withdrawal of the tenuous sufferance on which their participation was based.

This attitude was in direct contrast to the faculty and administration at Mount Holyoke and other women's colleges who tended to base their feminism on their sense of separateness from men. As separatists, Mary Woolley, Nellie Neilson, and their colleagues had rejected marriage as a trap for a professional woman. In some ways they were more sophisticated in assessing the impossibility of being accepted on equal terms with men. These women had seen the value, when necessary, of establishing separate institutions for women, and they also spent considerable energy in promoting their younger colleagues. Women like Dorothy Reed, on the other hand, were uncomfortable with this concentration on separatist strategies for women. They preferred to gravitate toward the exhilarating if elusive goal of merging themselves and their work with that of male colleagues, and to do this they had to minimize differences. They continued to believe that they would gain acceptance if only their professional performance was first rate.

Reed recalled with amusement bordering on disdain that M. Carey Thomas and the Baltimore Women's Committee, who had been so instrumental in forcing Johns Hopkins to accept women, were eager for her and her colleague Florence Sabin to march in the Johns Hopkins academic procession. The elder feminists "wanted the world to know that there were women on the Johns Hopkins University faculty—though she stretched it a bit to put two simple internes in high places."[26] Reed's attitude contrasted markedly with Thomas's view. The younger woman revealed an uncritical acceptance of the faculty hierarchy and was loathe to pass herself off as an equal. As a mere intern she felt outranked and inferior.

To a feminist like Thomas, the public spectacle of two women marching with an all-male faculty was a visible argument that they were more than tokens in that estimable institution. In Thomas's desire to see the two interns participate in an academic procession, she seized the occasion for a public reminder that there were in fact no women on the university faculty, nor even in the undergraduate student body. If Thomas and the committee had not previously intervened with their generous endowment gift, there would have been no women whatever in the medical school.

Although Reed had been one of the beneficiaries of the efforts of the Baltimore Women's Committee, she was not like the Mount Holyoke faculty who emulated and admired the strong women college presidents. Any gratitude she may have felt was vitiated by the personal repugnance with which she regarded feminist reformers like Thomas and Woolley.[27] Years later, when Reed met Carey Thomas again, she "was thankful that my life was not that of an administrator or pioneer in any profession for women." She believed that "being in the limelight continuously and exercising authority over the young and immature is a fearful responsibility and one that develops unpleasant characteristics."[28]

Reed seems to have lacked that sense of connection with other women that might have made her more charitable toward the excesses of their leadership. A different kind of woman might have understood that a shrill insistence on their authority was the occupational disease of some pathbreakers. Although Reed claimed many women friends, she confessed to not having one to "whom I ever felt like unburdening myself."[29] In this she differed from many other accomplished women, including Thomas and Woolley, who enjoyed lifelong, profound, and sustaining friendships with other women.[30] Still, Reed realized that her male friends could not be much help in that regard because she knew that the "problems of a man's life are so essentially different from those facing a woman that it would be difficult for him to put himself in her place and see the straight path." Usually, she ended by making decisions on her own and "prayed a lot" that her solitary choices would be the right ones.[31]

Even in her recollections in late life, Reed's ambivalence about herself as a woman is still discernable. In recalling her experience at Hopkins, she made the comforting generalization that "on the whole we women at Johns Hopkins were treated very well. Some over-attention while in school and a little horse play." Presumably their positions improved when they became interns, for she asserted that "there was no discrimination against us."[32] Yet she thought it important enough to record that the female interns at Hopkins did not go into the doctors' lounge in their rest periods but visited the nurses' sitting room because "46 years ago we still felt on sufferance and wished to be unobtrusive."[33] The ambiguity of these judgments becomes more apparent when, several pages later, she reconsidered once more and revised her view to include the reservation that "we were tolerated and on the whole treated well—but we were distinctly not wanted."[34]

These double messages about her acceptability as a physician became more noticeable when she finished medical school and applied for an internship at Johns Hopkins. Florence Sabin and Dorothy Reed were third and fourth in class rank respectively. William Osler, the head of Medicine, advised Reed that there were only four available internships in medicine, the most coveted specialty, and that he could not accept two women, even if their grades made them otherwise eligible. He suggested that Reed go into surgery or obstetrics, but these appointments were less desirable.

Armed with her belief that merit should count, Reed refused to compromise and encouraged the less assertive Sabin to do the same. In the end, they were both awarded the desired placements as interns in medicine, but not without some cost in colleagueship. Those who had ranked lower in the class proved jealous and put off by the fact that half the available places in medicine had been allocated to women.[35] To Reed, "this animosity was a blow. It was the first time that I personally was made to feel that I was not wanted in the medical profession and my first realization of the hard time any woman has to get recognition for equal work."[36]

This lesson learned early in her career was to be repeated in numerous settings. In her work as a doctor, Reed had to resist continually the powerful prejudices that forced most women to the margins of the medical profession. Unlike the professors at Mount Holyoke, she was never in a situation where women evaluated her performance or provided a reference group for those struggling for professional achievement. Throughout the course of her professional life Reed was forced to confront the special problems of women, holding fast to the conviction that talent would ultimately prevail.

Even when faced with prejudice clearly based on considerations other than ability, it was hard for Reed to surrender her belief in meritocracy. She, after all, had been admitted to one of the finest institutions in the United States on the same terms as male students. She and others like her could not help but observe that the

medical profession had demonstrated its own commitment to meritocratic ideas by upgrading the curriculum
and by providing an education that centered on scientific
and rational training. At Johns Hopkins claims to superiority were based on open, verifiable, objective criteria.
If excellence was the basis of the admissions policy for
students as well as for faculty appointments, then surely
demonstrating superior achievement would lead to recognition and success. Reed and her female contemporaries had imbibed these ideas along with their laboratory work. Optimistically, they believed that the fight to
admit women to the medical profession had been won.
Their internship experience did not always bear out this
optimism, however, and they continued to struggle
with a set of beliefs that did not always conform to the
evidence.[37]

In contrast, Emily Barringer was a female physician
who was forced to confront more directly women's unequal opportunity for professional advancement. When
she compared her situation with that of her future husband and other fellow medical students, she recalled that

> inevitably our long discussions emphasized fully how dif-
> ferent our horizons were going to be after graduation. He
> could count on a splendid training in one of the big hospi-
> tals with post-graduate work abroad in whatever line he
> elected—and I, what did I see ahead? Up to this time I had
> worked side by side with men and had shared the same
> work, responsibilities, and privileges, but as my gradua-
> tion approached, what might I hope for? Somehow my
> whole future began to close in and grow small just at a time
> when greater opportunities should be opening up. I found I

was becoming oppressed by the thoughts of my coming limitations and felt as the musician must feel who has practiced long and faithfully on his clavier to acquire and perfect his technique, only to be told at last that he may not try his skill on the Steinway grand piano. Surely it was illogical for the medical school to train women physicians equally with men, and then make no adequate arrangements for them to obtain internships.[38]

Furthermore, prejudice and humiliation did not end when the internships were secured. When Reed completed her internship, she applied for a fellowship in pathology. Her confirmation ran a rather different course than it would have had she been a male candidate. She was confirmed with only "a perfunctory question or two. Dr. Gildersleeve, Professor of Classics, rose and said before affirming [her] appointment he would like to ask Dr. Welch [dean of the medical faculty] one question, 'Was the candidate good looking?' The meeting broke up in confusion and with Dr. Welch all hot and bothered."[39]

Reed was less than confident about her role as a highly visible woman in a predominantly male institution. The young pathologist believed that she was always "conspicuous anyway as one of the few medical women employed in the medical school or hospital" and "felt often as if [she], too, were under the microscope."[40]

## MARRIAGE AND CAREER DISRUPTION

Dorothy Reed's sense of vulnerability to special scrutiny persisted well after her training and accounted for her decision to keep her impending marriage a secret from hospital superiors. She feared it would prompt unwanted comments about neglect of her work, presumably through some romantic distraction on her part.[41]

Reed's determination to keep this secret was only the first, and relatively minor, sign of the more radical career disruptions that were to result from her decision to marry. Already in her early thirties, she understood that marriage had consequences not only for her own career, but probably also for other women in succeeding generations, whose prospects for success would be determined by a judgment of her accomplishments.

Nevertheless, as she matured, the stability of married life increasingly appealed to her. A series of family deaths made the prospect of "a family and normal home life very attractive and necessary in that context of personal uncertainty."[42] In 1905, after a long courtship and considerable doubt on her part, she married Charles Mendenhall, a professor of physics at the University of Wisconsin. By this time she had achieved some professional success at leading hospitals both in Baltimore and in New York City. Dean William Welch had become very supportive of her work. On at least one occasion he had praised her publicly and "said as I closed [the lecture] that the audience had had the privilege of hearing a description by the leading authority on the [Hodgkins] disease," a subject for research that he had originally recommended to her.[43]

Her marriage appeared to turn Reed into a kind of apostate. Her mentors and some of her colleagues construed it as a rejection of professional commitment on her part. As a married woman, whenever she saw Welch, "usually in Washington at the meetings of the National Academy he always asked anxiously, 'Are you keeping up with your reading?'"[44] The reiteration of that patronizing question and the embarrassment that was repeated at professional meetings must have been very difficult for her. Behind that seemingly solicitous query was the unspoken accusation that she was wasting her training, which made her "suppose I was a great disappointment to him."[45]

Nor was she fully accepted by her husband's family. Her in-laws were not at all pleased that their son had decided to marry a doctor. "As far as the Mendenhalls were concerned, I was a professional woman—a type they disliked. Father Mendenhall never spoke of me or introduced me to anyone as a physician. Mrs. Mendenhall, always subservient to his every wish, was not the first vice-president of the Anti-Suffrage-Association for nothing. So I certainly was not wanted as an in-law."[46]

If these rejections were not sufficiently humiliating, she also learned that her marriage was used as justification for keeping women out of other medical schools. Dr. Alice Hamilton, the only female faculty member at Harvard Medical School, told Reed that she was cited as an example of a wasted education when the Harvard faculty debated the possibility of admitting female students. It was characteristic of that institution's determined efforts, successful until 1946, to keep themselves free of women that the faculty seized on Reed's example as "an able woman who had married and failed to use her expensive medical education."[47]

In Reed's thousand-page memoir there is nothing to

match the bristling anger of her comments on this particular point. She admitted that "it always hurt, but now I know it was a damn lie, and I can claim honestly that I think that I can give evidence of the use of medical knowledge much wider and deeper than that shown by the average physicians, whether in practice or teaching." And the elderly doctor, still smarting from the affronts of decades past, added for good measure, "This is why I am writing this section on my work after marriage."[48]

By any standards the work she engaged in after marriage was significant. In the early part of her career, Reed made significant discoveries about Hodgkins disease. She is also known for her work in public health—especially maternal and infant care—the interest she pursued when marriage and childbirth ended her research and hospital practice. Nevertheless, these accomplishments evoked an ill-concealed disdain from erstwhile colleagues. However painful such rejection, it encouraged a healthy skepticism in her toward their "expert advice" and judgment. Before her marriage, she had been fortunate to secure a rare staff position, one of a handful open to women, in a New York hospital. After she was married she was expected to leave that prestigious position and follow her husband and his work to Madison, Wisconsin—a small, medically backward town.[49] This had serious consequences for her professional life. She soon learned that the inadequacy of medical care would have a profound impact on her private welfare as well. Preparing to deliver her first child and only daughter, she had to remind the doctor to wash his hands before coming to the delivery table. This was a macabre turn of events for the sophisticated Hopkins graduate, supine and terrified, who later blamed the infant's death in parturition on the primitive obstetrical care.[50]

In Wisconsin during this period, male practitioners received rather questionable training. They did not welcome the competition of any woman, and Reed's superior education at Johns Hopkins did nothing to lessen their antagonism toward a better-trained competitor. When stresses of married life and her grief after her infant's death depressed her, she thought that professional work would provide her with much needed activity and a sense of purpose. At first she could only fantasize about returning to the East and taking up practice there. She writes that she "thought of it every day and made all sorts of plans" that were totally impossible if she wished to maintain her marriage.[51]

She remained with her husband in Wisconsin. Managing to forge some professional connections there, she moved into the most marginal professional areas— health education and hygiene. Most physicians had little interest in these areas, preferring to pursue the more lucrative path of treating the ill in private practice. Justifying professional lecture engagements on the grounds that she was badly in need of additional income to educate her sister's orphaned children, she took to the platform in the small, rural towns of Wisconsin to speak on basic nutrition, child care, and infectious diseases. Traveling in harsh midwestern winters to address a meeting of fifteen or twenty mothers was physically demanding, but she found this work exhilarating and personally rewarding, and it paid. She viewed it as "an answer to my prayers, for besides the money I made, it gave me a needed outlet and a way back into professional work."[52]

This activity was a far cry from the fee-for-service, one-on-one medical practice of her male colleagues and at the opposite end of the professional spectrum from the research work of her Hopkins mentors. Yet because she was not welcome in these mainstream activities, she went to work in marginal areas of the medical profession. Through this work she developed a critical stance about some of the conventional paths to professional success. Her new career, which culminated in twenty years of service for the Children's Bureau, a newly formed federal agency, focused on issues of public health. The work of the agency was theoretically and ideologically at odds with conventional private medical practice. This did not deter Reed from eagerly seeking out such a position when her husband relocated in Washington, D.C., during the First World War. She was already working in the most marginal areas and had few vested interests to protect.

A paper Reed wrote titled "Prenatal and Natal Conditions in Wisconsin" typified the nature of the work and the aims of her career in public health. It dealt with infant mortality in childbirth and illustrated both the subject of her developing interests and the adversarial role that public health women professionals began to take toward their male colleagues in private practice. At that time, physicians rather glibly blamed the high incidence of puerperal deaths (5.6 per thousand) on the participation of female midwives and nurses, whom they claimed were not trained to handle deliveries in a modern scientific fashion that would avoid childbed fever. It was partly a measure of Reed's exclusion from the mainstream network of physicians that allowed her to proclaim forthrightly a different and discomforting conclusion: the high infant mortality rate was more the fault of the physicians than any other group involved in childbirth attendance. She went on to insist that the preventive measures advocated by the Children's Bureau— visiting nurse services, nutritional education, sensible prenatal care—were critical to the health of the mother and the baby.

This view appeared especially radical because physicians increasingly espoused disease theory and generally ignored preventive prenatal and postnatal care. They also rejected natural childbirth techniques in favor of forceps and similar interventionist methods that allowed them to apply new technologies and demonstrate their individual expertise. These new techniques may have made their presence at birthing seem more indispensable, but it also tended to put mother and child at risk.[53] Reed's research had made her more cynical about their claims to expertise. Her data showed, she insisted, that their methods were responsible for the high death rates and that though the "shoe fitted the doctors did not want to put it on." Not surprisingly, her paper was received with little enthusiasm when she read it at the seventieth annual meeting of the Wisconsin State Medical Society.[54]

Reed realized that being a "woman and from the east" also played a part in the cold reception she received from the doctors at the Madison meeting. Moreover, "public health work was new to most physicians and seemed to the majority of the profession in Madison a distinct effort to undermine their means of livelihood."[55] This market competition, which tended to intrude on the more noble aims that the profession publicly espoused, was confirmed privately by some of the more forthright physicians. One of her colleagues, a Dr. Harper, who was also secretary of the local board of health, pointed out to her that she "was wrong in considering that medicine was a profession when it was really a business."[56]

Despite many disclaimers from medical spokesmen, this unvarnished self-interest was prevalent among the aspiring and upwardly mobile groups that comprised the profession in the early twentieth century. Dr. S. Josephine Baker reported on the testimony of a male physician who was representing a New England medical society before a congressional committee hearing, which was

> considering the appropriation of funds for the newly founded Federal Children's Bureau. I was down there testifying too—on the other side. This New England doctor actually got up and told the committee: "We oppose this bill because, if you are going to save the lives of all these women and children at public expense, what inducement will there be for young men to study medicine?" Senator Sheppard, the chairman, stiffened and leaned forward: "Perhaps I didn't understand you correctly," he said; "You surely don't mean that you want women and children to die unnecessarily or live in constant danger of sickness so there will be something for young doctors to do?" "Why

not?" said the New England doctor, who did at least have the courage to admit the issue; "That's the will of God, isn't it?"[57]

Baker's comments were significant not only for what they revealed about the values of some physicians, but also for what she unmasked about the structure of the profession. The medical establishment set goals for practitioners that emphasized the mastery of disease theory, the commitment to interventionist treatment, and fee-for-service patient interaction; these goals were touted by doctors at the top of the professional hierarchy. On the other hand, women doctors like Reed, excluded from the medical elite, often supported community public health, emphasized preventive treatment, and enthusiastically endorsed the benefits of health education for all classes. For the women involved, the creation of health agencies widened opportunities. Although Reed never surrendered her belief in merit as the best way for professional women to succeed, her active and long-term association with public health work represented her adoption of an additional strategy—innovative response—to overcome discrimination.

In forging public health agencies, women physicians were creating a very different model of treatment. Their concerns were more comprehensive and their style of organization more collective. This kind of public enterprise gave women like Dorothy Reed the flexibility to mesh more easily the demands of their personal and professional lives. Public health also provided an arena where it was acceptable for a woman to be ambitious because her work ameliorated the suffering of the poor, who were largely ignored by the conventional practitioners. Most male leaders of the profession considered this kind of service an inferior endeavor, barely made respectable by its altruistic goals. Reed began her career as a superperformer committed to progress by extraordinary achievement in male-dominated institutions. She found herself, in time, among the innovators, creating a new career in public health.

If it was downgraded by the medical establishment, this work was supported by a generation of female settlement house workers and social reformers whose enthusiasm for the female physicians' services was unbounded. Julia Lathrop, that indefatigable head of the Children's Bureau, was eager to have a woman such as Reed on her staff because she had a double set of credentials. As a married woman with children, Reed justified, through personal and direct experience, the public concern with the improvement of maternal and child care. As a doctor she could offer impeccable qualifications in testifying before congressional committees or making other kinds of public appearances. S. Josephine Baker, the eminent director of the first Bureau of Child Hygiene in New York City, recounts similar appreciation for her title of M.D.: "I was always going down to testify at hearings on Children's Bureau appropriations because Miss Julia Lathrop, the Bureau's brilliant first chief, thought I was a good ally. I was called Doctor instead of Miss and so could escape from the eternal remark always coming up among Congressmen about giving money to an old maid to spend."[58]

As the work of the Children's Bureau and its physicians became better known, women's accomplishments
as professional physicians became increasingly suspect
by those who represented private physicians. Dorothy
Reed described the growing antagonism when she recalled that the "medical profession (with few exceptions) belittled all the work of the Children's Bureau and
questioned our statistics, or at least our presentation of
them." [59] She, in turn, expressed her displeasure with
male practitioners by refusing to join the local branch of
the powerful American Medical Association (AMA).
This gesture had little impact on the goals of the AMA—
it was the recourse of a marginal person and tended only
to confirm her lack of affiliation and her status as a professional outcast. In retrospect, Reed decided that this
action might have been a tactical error because it rendered
her powerless to challenge the leadership whom she de-
tested. [60] In fact, though, even if she and like-minded
women had become members, there were not enough
women in the profession to have provided sufficient leverage to influence any of the policies of the AMA. Reed
underestimated the obdurate resistance that any real female incursion would have provoked, to say nothing of
the reaction to any challenge posed by those women
who had created the public health movement, which the
AMA disliked so intensely. [61]

Dorothy Reed herself acknowledged the connections
between her personal experience and her professional
choices. Her work at the Children's Bureau focused almost exclusively on maternity issues. She believed that
the "tragic death of my first child, Margaret, from bad

obstetrics in 1907, was the dominant factor in my interest in the chief function of women."[62] It was not atypical for the married woman professional to justify her professional work in highly personal and maternal terms. In the same vein, Reed viewed the "Child Health Centers of Madison," which she was instrumental in founding, as "a monument to my boy Richard [who died accidentally at age two], all the writing and teaching on safe maternity, I have thought of as memorial to Margaret, my first child and only girl." She ended that touching recollection with an underscored and revealing observation that "*a mother never forgets.*"[63]

This line represents something more than the unique sentiment of a particular mother's grief. It appears to be more than coincidence that Anne Walter Fearn, whose career pattern was totally different, also attributed her interest in working with children to the death of her only daughter at age five. In her memoirs Fearn suggests that "If Elizabeth's visit with us had not been so brief I might have been content to relinquish my practice and stay at home. I do not know."[64]

Yet, there is nothing to indicate that she would have retired from practice if her daughter had lived, nor did she seem to enjoy curtailing her activity while her daughter was still alive. What is significant is that both women seemed to believe that they had to justify their work as something more than conventional professional engagement by elevating it to a kind of memorial to their deceased children.

Yet in other ways Anne Walter Fearn's career differs substantially from that of Dorothy Reed. Fearn's represented the professional style of combining marriage and family in a quasi-institutional setting—a departure that permitted a more egalitarian relationship with her husband and gave her somewhat wider professional options.

Anne Walter (Fearn) was a southern debutante who was given a fashionable coming-out party at the governor's mansion in Jackson, Mississippi.[65] When this proper young belle announced to her family that she intended to study medicine, they were horrified because "Dr. Mary Walker in gentlemen's attire was our idea of a woman doctor," and she was considered to be "a sacrilege against womanhood."[66] Mrs. Walter wired her daughter who was visiting in California, where a woman physician was encouraging her to become a professional, to consider that "No disgrace has yet fallen upon your father's name. Should you persist in carrying out your mad determination to study medicine I shall never again recognize you as my daughter."[67]

The girl's previous behavior appears to have been quite unremarkable. In fact, the young socialite's career decision led a physician friend of the family to observe that "as a social butterfly Miss Walter would be a great success, as a physician never—there is nothing to her."[68] Apparently, there was little indication at that stage that she would persist in her goal and ultimately found and administer a hospital in China.[69]

This unusual woman, whose family had expected her to live the conventional life of a wealthy southern wife, instead prevailed upon them to use their influence to obtain a place for her in the Women's Medical College of Pennsylvania. Her prominent family obtained reference letters for her from her "father's friends, Governor Stone, Governor Robert Lowry, and one or two others." A friend of hers, Dr. Elizabeth Yates, assisted her financially at the medical college, and Fearn later named her only daughter after this early supporter.[70]

Fearn describes her student experience in the very different female environment of Pennsylvania as largely positive. She became the protégé of Joseph Price, "a Southerner and one of the world's greatest surgeons and obstetricians." He took "a fancy" to her and "had unlimited faith in my future success." In the fashion of the late nineteenth century, Price had his own hospital, the Preston Retreat, "one of the largest maternity hospitals in the United States." Fearn served as his nurse and assistant and received a valuable apprenticeship.[71] Pursuing a more traditional form of education than Reed's, Fearn did not go to college and received much of her education as an apprentice.

When she finished medical school, and following a period of apprenticeship in a major maternity hospital, Fearn seemed unclear about the shape her career would take. She decided to leave for China to see what medical practice there would be like. She viewed her decision to go with youthful casualness—as "a wonderful chance for me to see the world"—but the decision came as "a shock" to her mother. The young doctor was careful to point out to family and friends that she would "not go as a missionary." As in the case of a good many late-nineteenth-century professional women, religious commitment was not the driving force in her work. She recalled with some satisfaction that she had announced she was not a missionary, "not even a church member"; rather she insisted, "I'm a physician."[72] By 1893 she had begun her work in China at the Soochow Woman's Hospital. Originally the hospital had been organized by another female physician, Mildred Phillips, who left when she married. The facility had been forced to close for lack of staff, but when the young southern doctor arrived, it was reopened.[73]

Within a few years, she had met and married Dr. John Burrus Fearn. Like Dorothy Reed in Wisconsin, marriage and geography had an impact on her career. Since her husband was a missionary, their marriage "definitely settled my fate as far as my return to the United States was concerned, for my husband expected to make China the field for his life work; as for me I had grown to love the country so well that I welcomed the prospect of exile."[74]

On the surface the young couple appeared compatible in many ways. He, too, was a Southerner; they had both been raised in neighboring Mississippi towns. Despite this common background, their marriage was marked by dissension and conflict from their earliest days together. According to Fearn, the source of their difficulty was the fact that "my husband had grown up in the Church. I had not. For every hour he had spent in Sunday School and church I had spent two in dancing and similar pleasure."[75] In many ways his austere Christianity was repugnant to his wife.

But the fact that she did not share his religious preoccupation could not alone account for their estrangement. Her own evidence indicates that it was not her desire for "pleasure" that was at the core of their disaffection, but rather something quite different and perhaps more divisive—her commitment to work. She tells us that she "honestly endeavored to follow his wishes. . . . one of his obsessions was that the day should begin with prayer and Bible reading, and that the Bible should be read through methodically once or twice a year." None of this was especially aberrant for a missionary and would hardly have been unusual for a conventional wife of that period. But it made Fearn late for rounds and hence interfered with her care of her patients.

One morning, when the pressure of work seemed particularly acute, she lost control, seized the Bible, threw it to the floor, and rushed out of the room screaming "I wish I'd never seen the damned thing."[76] The upshot was that "this little flare-up ended the Bible readings." The subject was never mentioned again, but her husband "never forgave nor forgot, and I lost forever my taste, if I ever had any, for the Old Testament."[77]

Within the first year of their marriage she became pregnant; also, her husband was transferred to a different assignment. She followed him there, but she returned to Soochow to deliver her child in the facility that she "had built in the compound of the Women's Hospital."[78] After several years their child died. The family returned to the United States for a brief furlough together. Subsequently her husband accepted employment with the Associate Protestant Mission in China and was reassigned, this time to Shanghai.

Fearn viewed the change with little enthusiasm, for "after the first excitement of settling a new home had subsided I found that I missed Soochow and my own work with a poignancy that made me restless and dissatisfied."[79] Further depressed by the prospect that "a period of apparently endless drifting was opening for me, although I was never without some work to do," she tried to combine volunteer and charity work as a substitute for full-time professional employment. Her husband became the chief financial support of the family; she undertook the role of housewife and active volunteer. "For several years I was to expend my energy on various activities without finding the one channel into which they could flow with complete satisfaction. It was a new experience for me and not wholly a happy one."[80]

When World War I broke out, Fearn wanted to move into a more demanding life. She tried to enlist in the Red Cross, but this organization accepted only female nurses or male doctors. This rejection was a great disappointment because she had been looking forward to working as a physician once again. The past few years in Shanghai had not given her the opportunity to "practice medicine in good earnest," although that had been her intention. She worked at a local clinic several hours each day. But neither this nor her American Women's Club activities could fill her day or ease the "rankling sensation that something more important, to me at least, lay waiting around the corner; and I must find it or remain forever only half a person."[81]

Although the Red Cross failed to offer her new professional opportunities, the war did have far-reaching consequences for the Fearns' personal lives. John Fearn was called to serve as a physician in France. In his absence Anne Fearn set up her own hospital, although she apparently did this with some trepidation, for she was aware that

> all of our married life was tinged by the merest shadow of professional jealousy. He had a strong sense of masculine protectiveness . . . and he was never so completely himself as when helping the sick and the weak. But in marrying a woman who took life with both hands and people as she found them, this protective instinct was more or less frustrated. He would much rather have had his wife sit at home and be managed by him.[82]

Yet at the same time she concluded that "for her devotion to duty as a doctor, however, he had only admiration." It was his "admiration" she was counting on, after his return, to gain his acceptance of her continued operation of her own hospital. His acceptance, she reported with some satisfaction, was mixed with ambivalence as they became "rivals in good earnest."[83]

When he returned, he assumed the superintendency of the Shanghai General Hospital. Fearn continued to work at her own hospital and to maintain her own apartment there, though she slept in his living quarters at his hospital, she tells us, in part because this provided a change of scene for her. From her husband's point of view, this arrangement had some obvious drawbacks. Despite his "admiration" of her work as a doctor, he "condemned my lack of interest in the religious life, and felt that my independence was unbecoming to a woman."[84] She did add, with some relief, that in 1926 he forgave her, on his death bed, for opening the hospital because she had given care and comfort to the sick.

When Dr. Fearn finally left her hospital it was with great reluctance, remarking that "it was the last day of a decade spent in the beloved hospital-home."[85] She claimed that she closed it because a newer facility had opened that provided similar service, and her husband's failing health made it more and more difficult to continue her work. She was not prepared to admit that her decision was made principally because of her subordination to her husband's needs, but that appears to have been the case.

Establishing her own hospital had been the high point of Fearn's life. It was made possible by the special circumstances of life in China and by the institutional setting that the hospital-home provided. If she had been living in the United States, the medical establishment would not easily have let her institute her own facility or assume sole control of its management. Her innovative response to these constraints resembled that of other women in medicine, who moved to places where there was little competition from men and certainly none from the American medical establishment. But even the exotic circumstances of the Orient did little to change the conventional expectations of her husband, whose wishes she frequently challenged with some success and always with considerable ambivalence. Yet having embarked on her own project while he was in France during the war, she continued it after his return. In some ways the separateness of their work lives probably alleviated as much conflict as it engendered.

Married women who practiced medicine, like Anne Fearn, always faced the suspicion of others. In part, these women reacted by emphasizing the humanitarian and altruistic dimensions of their medical practices. Women's special role in alleviating misery, much reiterated, was bolstered by the definition of medicine as a "sacred" activity that sustained the value of life. But the sacred was understood to have two dimensions: one was the discovery and penetration of the mysteries of life through the implementation of the scientific method; the other was its altruistic component. The most eminent male practitioners had already arrogated the first by monopolizing control of the medical schools, the teaching hospitals, and the scholarly journals.[86]

The second dimension of the sacred, "an ideal of service and devotion to human welfare," was left for female practitioners and their supporters as a major goal.[87] Their appropriation of this exclusive and elevated concern was necessary in order to legitimize their intrusion into sacrosanct areas of physiological functioning, areas that men claimed as their exclusive territory.[88]

Fearn's commitment to the noble cause of healing probably placated her missionary husband's worst resentment. But in the end, it was he who forgave her for devoting her life to alleviating the misery of the sick. Female professionals, like Fearn, often felt that they should explain and try to legitimize their professional ambitions and goals. To do this they frequently referred to their dedication to service, with its "feminine" tone of caring. But these explanations rarely satisfied those who were critical of their dedication to their work.

Fearn and Reed shared more than their marital status. In both cases their professional goals put a serious strain on their relations with their husbands. Both women had married after they had embarked on their professional careers, which meant that their husbands knowingly selected professional spouses. Extant evidence reflects only the wives' assessments of their husbands' personalities and only their views of the marriage relationship. By their accounts, it appears that these men were unusual for their time in their willingness to choose wives who did not fit traditional expectations. Yet in other ways they emerge in the wives' portrayals as very conventional, late Victorian men. For example, Reed describes her husband's suspicion of pleasure by recalling that "when I married him, Charles had never danced, smoked, played cards, or indulged in any of the usual pastimes of youth . . . what was really true was that his straight-laced upbringing had made him question every harmless pleasure—if he enjoyed a thing he had a feeling it must be wrong."[89] Here and elsewhere she implies that he was passive and lacked the engagement with life that marked her own personality. Fearn made similar observations.[90]

Although it is impossible from the surviving evidence to separate personal tensions and professional frustrations, both women's memoirs recount at great length the dissensions in their conjugal relationships. The women vacillate between expressing their hostility to their husbands and punishing themselves in guilty confessions of wifely inadequacies. A quarter of a century after Charles Mendenhall's death, his wife was still debating the

wisdom of her decision to marry him in terms that re-
flect the complexity of her feelings.

> There had been several times, especially in the Spring of
> 1904, which it seemed impossible for me to carry on the
> arrangement [engagement] or to think of marriage with
> him or any man. Gradually Charles' devotion, tenderness
> for me and innate goodness conquered my doubts. . . . I
> felt that I could go through with it and with his help and
> understanding make him a fairly decent wife. I have always
> had my doubts, if it were fair to him.[91]

Another section of her autobiography records:

> Neither the years before I was married, or those of my early
> married life were happy ones and yet I struggled through
> them, and after 1917 I worked out a way of living and a plan
> for the boys' training and education that gave me satisfac-
> tion at the time and has made the early decades of 1900
> seem worthwhile—in spite of the agony.[92]

It is of course extremely difficult to generalize about
the quality of marriage in a given society. Surely there
were unhappy marriages between conventional wives
and husbands. A number of scholars have concluded that
the many ailments found among middle-class married
women, such as neuresthenia, hysteria, and back problems, probably can be attributed to dissatisfaction with
their domestic lives.[93] What distinguishes these two physicians is their willingness to write so frankly about their
anger and frustration. It is equally noteworthy that they
did not succumb to the common recourse to hypo-

chondria and invalidism, but drew on the emotional resources that allowed them to develop as professionals and also as autonomous women.

Although the careers of Anne Walter Fearn and Dorothy Reed Mendenhall differed substantially, several important similarities shed light on the female professional experience and especially on their role as innovators. As married women, they succeeded in their professional lives by carrying out work among remote or socially subordinate clients. Their work was neither unworthy nor unnecessary; indeed, in the long run it probably had a greater social impact than most private practices. But those in the medical establishment who interpreted professional reality chose to define that work as inferior and less deserving of reward. Like most women, these two physicians were excluded from the powerful, financially rewarding, and prestigious positions.

It is also clear that the complications of their marriages impeded their careers. Whereas marriage and family supported and sustained men's professional endeavors and augmented their chances for success, for women marriage was an obstacle to conventional standards of achievement. Marriage was a central factor in the female life cycle for Reed and Fearn, as for others; but for them it also became a barrier to achievement because it made demands on their time and energy that were incompatible with their professional expectations. Since home and work were viewed as irreconcilable obligations, women ordinarily had to choose one or the other. Reed and Fearn defied these conventions and insisted on doing both.

To meet both sets of demands often required the adoption of more than one strategy over the life cycle. Early in their careers, both tended to emphasize superperformance in order to prove their competence as physicians. Later, they were also eager to demonstrate their equal capacities as excellent mothers and wives. When they found themselves with no regular employment or only mundane volunteer work, they added a new strategy: innovative response. Each carved out meaningful work in special circumstances outside the mainstream of the profession. This strategy offered a reasonable answer to their professional problems, although it never fully satisfied their private conflicts. Pursuit of these new careers did not always mesh well with the subordinate status expected of a wife. Instead, both women maintained an uneasy balance between their public and private lives without ever resolving the tensions that marriage and medicine evoked.

Despite the conflicts and personal turmoil, Reed and Fearn never sacrificed their commitment to merit and service as the hallmarks of professionalism. Early in their training they had learned that medicine combined scientific and intellectual achievement with a sacred devotion to healing. Throughout their work lives they remained loyal to these goals, despite the fact that their work was often evaluated by family and peers on other grounds.

Women's achievements were often unwelcome because they endangered the exclusivity of the male monopoly or, as in the case of the Madison physicians, threatened male physicians' own claims to expertise. Similarly, women doctors such as Fearn and Reed frequently called upon the ideology of service to justify their work as a legitimate female activity. Yet this commitment to heal the sick never adequately countered their husbands' demands on their time and energies. Often they were left with feelings of ambivalence and guilt despite their substantial achievements.

Commitment to service remained problematic for women professionals in the decades to come. They worked diligently to prove their competence and commitment, but failed to realize fully that professional acceptance did not depend on achievement alone.[94] Full acceptance required political organization and leverage, which struggling isolated women could rarely achieve alone. Only in a more supportive setting could these ambitious women have hoped to pave the way for the next generation of professionals, so that those younger women would not have to face all the battles of exclusion and prejudice anew.

# THE PROMISE OF NEW OPPORTUNITIES IN SCIENCE

Modern scientific research took a gigantic leap forward during the first two decades of the twentieth century. As several wealthy philanthropists invested substantial sums of money to establish modern laboratories and research institutes, unprecedented opportunities in medical research opened up and educated women joined their male colleagues in seeking careers in biological and medical research. In the same year other female scientists embarked on a different style of research, one that emphasized fieldwork and the slow incremental collection of empirical and statistical data; it was pursued by those interested in public health, industrial medicine, and the reform of industrial society.

The laboratory style, carried out in an environment that stressed a value-free posture, was more experimental and more quantitative than field research. This style would soon become the dominant mode of scientific research. Women thrived in this atmosphere at first, but subsequently experienced severe setbacks. The field research style was much more connected to social ends. Data were collected in urban slums and on factory floors rather than in the laboratory. Sometimes the work involved great personal risks and was usually fueled by a greater political consciousness. Many women gravitated to this type of research because of its links to social ser-

## NEW OPPORTUNITIES IN SCIENCE

vice and settlement houses, areas where women had worked in substantial numbers for several decades.

To explain how women, after a promising beginning, were increasingly excluded from positions of leadership in scientific research, we will examine the lives of two of the most successful researchers: Florence R. Sabin and Alice Hamilton. Sabin's life is worth examining in some detail because she was the most famous woman scientist of her generation; her case provides an opportunity to analyze her success and to assess under what conditions the strategies she employed were transferable to other women. Her career will also be compared with other female researchers at the Rockefeller Institute who were accomplished scientists but never achieved the national recognition that Sabin did.

Born in 1869 in Colorado, Florence R. Sabin graduated from Smith College and enrolled in the fourth class at Johns Hopkins Medical School. She remained at Hopkins from 1896 until 1925, first as a student, then as an intern and researcher, and then as the first female faculty member. Well known for her work on the lymphatic system, she was also an outstanding teacher. In 1925 she left her post as full professor and was appointed to a distinguished research position at the prestigious Rockefeller Institute for Medical Research. After her retirement she returned to Colorado where she served on several

Opposite: Florence R. Sabin, 1919. Florence Sabin Papers. Courtesy of Sophia Smith Collection, Women's History Archive, Smith College.

commissions and was instrumental in reforming the state's public health laws.[1]

Alice Hamilton was also an outstanding achiever. If Sabin's career illustrates the laboratory style of research, however, Hamilton's work demonstrates how field research developed at the turn of the century. Born in 1869, she was trained as a physician at the University of Michigan Medical School and did graduate work in science in Germany and at Johns Hopkins. After a brief sojourn in teaching and laboratory research, she moved into an area of scientific research largely shunned by the most ambitious and talented men: she became the nation's leading expert in lead poisoning and wrote several books on toxicology. This work led to her appointment as the first female faculty member at Harvard University. Her extraordinary contributions during her long lifetime ultimately brought her national recognition.[2]

Taken together, the careers of Hamilton and Sabin illustrate particular strategies and abilities that led to outstanding personal success. At the same time they reveal the obstacles women faced in trying to create possibilities for the next generation of female scientists and researchers.

## THE NEW SCIENCE

Women such as Sabin and Hamilton represented a real break with a long tradition of women scientists.

Opposite: Alice Hamilton, c. 1919. Courtesy of Schlesinger Library, Radcliffe College.

Throughout the nineteenth century, women had congregated in amateur scientific societies, where they gathered to discuss the papers of naturalists or to engage in systematic observations in a variety of fields. Women contributed a good deal to the growing interest in the categorization of plants, birds, and other animals. But by the end of the century rapid changes and a trend toward professionalism raised serious questions about their future in science. Women were frequently reminded that new developments in higher education represented a reorganization of the male-dominated public sphere that was not meant to include them. Sally Kohlstedt, in her study of women in science, notes that "participation at meetings, presentation of research papers, and public visibility, increasingly important professional activities, seemed a violation of established social norms for women."[3]

Women who were serious about careers in science quickly recognized that if they remained in small amateur societies, they would find themselves increasingly distant from developments in the field. Instead, sharing the new enthusiasm for careers in science, they sought professional training and graduate degrees. They went to the most modern graduate schools, which emphasized empirical, laboratory research in a style modeled on the most advanced German teaching methods. They would still have to compensate for the strong prejudicial claims that women were unlikely to equal men in conceptual ability, but scientific research was essentially a new field and many of the boundaries were more fluid for them than for women who entered medicine or law.

## NEW OPPORTUNITIES IN SCIENCE

Often women who wished to pursue careers in research received their initial undergraduate training at one of the women's colleges. Professors such as Lydia Marie Shattuck and Cornelia Clapp, naturalists at Mount Holyoke, and Maria Mitchell, who developed offerings in mathematics and astronomy at Vassar, were significant figures in the training of women. These teachers urged young female students to believe that they could be professional scientists and to reject the social norms that urged them to get married and have babies. Women's colleges, then, became feeders for graduate education and professional research when opportunities began to develop in that emerging field. By the beginning of the twentieth century, a small but determined number of women were seeking graduate training in the sciences.[4]

With doctoral degrees from Cornell, Columbia, or Stanford, or medical degrees from Johns Hopkins or Michigan, often supplemented with graduate work in Germany,[5] the first crop of female researchers amply demonstrated women's capacity to think scientifically and to work productively as members of the scientific community. Good graduate training, however, was not enough. To have successful research careers the women needed to find employment in settings that would allow access to necessary materials and financial support, as well as the challenge and encouragement of a network of colleagues.[6] So, of course, did men. But once out of school and into the professional world of employment, women's experiences proved to be quite different from those of male counterparts.

Florence Sabin, by dint of her outstanding ability, her

total dedication, and especially her excellent relationship with her mentor, Franklin Mall, was able to work in male scientific centers all of her life. Many of her contemporaries, in contrast, found that their careers could develop only in special female-designated areas. A brief consideration of scientific opportunities for women reveals the barriers Sabin overcame—a victory for herself and for future generations.

Margaret Rossiter has shown that as science expanded between 1880 and 1910, it was marked by a segregated labor market for women.[7] She distinguishes three kinds of positions for female scientists. First, with the rise of "big science" there was a hungry market for assistants at research centers. Directors of laboratories found that women worked for less money, did not compete with men, and were willing to stay on painstaking and detailed tasks for long periods of time. Astronomy became the archtype for this pattern of employment. Several important astronomy projects were completed with female labor, and the role of female assistants became well established even when the actual work performed did not differ substantially from that of their mentors, who ordinarily directed the research. By 1900 the Harvard astronomy department employed twenty female assistants, a model emulated at other major observatories.

Some women supported this subordinate form of employment, including the world famous astronomer Maria Mitchell, who apparently believed that it was important to find nonteaching jobs for women.[8] Although this practice did provide positions for women, the career path of the female research assistant was problematic.[9]

Women who worked in these positions rarely received salary increases and were not promoted even when they produced extraordinary work.

Second, there were jobs in plant physiology. During a period of rapid expansion in botany, the government employed significant numbers of scientific assistants. What specific circumstances accounted for the feminization of certain fields, such as plant physiology, is not clear, but Rossiter documents the ways in which certain publications signaled that particular fields were suitable for women.

Third, female nutritionists and chemists were channeled into special home economics departments. Diverted from the "hard" sciences into applied domestic studies, these women were virtually the only ones admitted to the faculties of coeducational colleges and universities. Despite some initial promise that home economics would concentrate on human nutrition, while biology focused on animal research, it quickly became evident that home economics was to play second string to chemistry and biology.

Beyond these three sex-segregated fields, another fact is apparent. Whenever women scientists were hired in regular science departments, they were rarely appointed to regular faculty rank unless they were employed in the women's colleges. The few who did have regular, tenured positions in coeducational institutions were highly visible tokens who hoped to lower barriers and make the presence of women scientists more acceptable in the future.[10]

The trend toward professionalization of science did not

eliminate qualified women from the pool of trained specialists with appropriate credentials. In fact, it is now clear that the absolute numbers of female Ph.D.s continued to grow steadily throughout the century, although the proportion declined when men began to enter science in large numbers.[11] Like female physicians, women scientists began to face the most formidable prejudice after they had completed their training and sought employment and opportunities for career development. It was at this point that most women found themselves in a highly segregated, and usually subordinate, labor market.

## BREAKING THE BARRIERS

Florence R. Sabin graduated from Smith College in 1893 and, after a brief period of work, entered the fourth class at Johns Hopkins where she achieved a brilliant record, graduating third in her class. Despite some initial resistance, she and her very able classmate, Dorothy Reed, were awarded the most coveted and prestigious internships in the medical department at Hopkins. Subsequently, Sabin began work as a research fellow in Franklin Mall's anatomy laboratory and remained there until 1925.[12]

Before graduating from medical school, Sabin had constructed a model of the brain stem of the newborn infant which contributed to the fundamental understanding of the structure of the brain. The book of drawings and descriptions that followed, *Atlas of the Medulla and the Mid-brain,* became a classic text in medical schools throughout the country.[13]

## NEW OPPORTUNITIES IN SCIENCE

The same Baltimore Women's Committee that had been so outspoken in insisting that women be accepted at Hopkins Medical School when it opened was now equally determined to open research positions to women.[14] The committee persuaded Mall to offer the young Sabin a fellowship in his laboratory and provided the $800 stipend to make it possible.[15] Once appointed, Sabin developed techniques for injecting dyes into specimens that allowed new methods of studying the lymphatic system. Publication of "Origin of the Lymphatic System" established her reputation as a researcher. As a result of this achievement, Franklin Mall convinced the authorities at Hopkins to break all precedents and give Sabin a regular appointment in his department when her fellowship expired.[16] She remained there as a research assistant and then research associate for several years. In 1907 she was appointed associate professor of anatomy. There was some discussion between Mall and Dean Welch about appointing her to the faculty, but by then both were persuaded of her exceptional talents.[17] She became a much loved teacher who trained generations of medical students in sophisticated laboratory skills. At the same time, she continued her own work on the lymphatic system.

In 1925 after twenty-nine years in Baltimore, she left to become the only woman appointed as a full member at the Rockefeller Institute for Medical Research. Most of her research efforts there focused on tuberculosis. Like many who spent a lifetime attempting to conquer this dreaded disease, Sabin made some inroads in understanding the process of inflammation of cells, but years of research produced no further significant results. Ultimately this work was put aside when antibiotics were discovered to be the most effective way to combat tuberculosis. After her retirement she returned to her native Colorado where she played an outstanding public role in upgrading the public health program of that state.[18]

Sabin's brilliant career did not progress unimpeded. In 1917, after spending fifteen years in the anatomy department as associate to Mall, she was passed over as his obvious successor in favor of a man whom many close to the scene considered "her inferior in age, experience, brains, and ability to succeed."[19] A number of Sabin's close associates were appalled. Franklin Mall's family believed that he had fully expected her to succeed him. His wife, herself a former student in the medical school, stated that "it was only the lingering prejudice against women that prevented Sabin's well-merited advancement."[20] Students petitioned and alumni expressed great surprise, but to no avail.[21]

What was the significance of this institutional failure to recognize and promote this woman scientist? Sabin herself chose to make no public statements about the action, but instead absorbed herself in her work. If her research continued to go well, she believed she would somehow achieve the recognition she deserved. Whatever her private disappointment, her publicly expressed faith in merit and achievement did not fade. What is clear is that many of her friends thought that she would never have accepted the Rockefeller appointment if she had not been cut off in her advancement at Hopkins. Others perceived the situation in broader terms—as a setback for the struggling group of women slowly advancing in the field.

## NEW OPPORTUNITIES IN SCIENCE

Her former classmate Dorothy Reed was aghast when she heard the news. A few years later Reed was entertaining the president of Johns Hopkins at her home in Wisconsin when he made a slighting remark about Sabin. She had left, he implied, for a larger salary at Rockefeller, after they had done so much for her. Reed, in her own words, "blew up and told him that Florence Sabin had been overlooked" and that an inferior man "was promoted over her." She further informed the president that "I should have had no respect for her if she had knuckled under."[22] Undoubtedly, the politically astute members of the Baltimore Women's Committee were equally repelled by the decision. It had taken considerable money and effort on their part to create opportunities for women in science, and Sabin's treatment represented a setback, notwithstanding her subsequent successful career at the Rockefeller Institute.

Sabin's commitment to her work clearly was powerful. She never married, and she had few personal distractions. Both of Sabin's biographers go to some pains to link her spinsterhood to her homely appearance. As is typical in discussions of unmarried women, these unflattering comments were coupled with some reference to her "beautiful, competent hands" or to her "vibrant personality."[23] But a woman's appearance, particularly a famous and accomplished woman of Florence Sabin's stature, was very apt to provoke comment, particularly when she remained unmarried. The widespread assumption was that an attractive woman had more opportunities to marry and would no doubt choose family life over professional activity.

In fact, recent research has documented the low marriage rates of women in many of the professions. Surveys show that in the first quarter of the century only a minority married. Married women often found themselves barred from holding jobs; many single women believed that even the possibility of marriage increased career risk.[24] Certainly, Sabin had to be aware of the career sacrifices that had accompanied Dorothy Reed's decision to marry and have children.[25]

Whatever the actual motives behind Sabin's decision to remain single, her commitment to professional life was never in doubt. We are assured that "she was a model of how a young lady should conduct herself in medical school," which meant that the "focus of attention was never on Dr. Sabin herself but always on the work at hand. The question of her standing out as a woman never arose."[26]

These qualities of physical plainness and personal diffidence, it may be argued, should have enhanced her career success; they might have made her the perfect candidate for equal professional treatment. She was brilliant, hardworking, self-effacing, and physically undistracting, the kind of no-nonsense professional of whom a former student would say, "What she repeatedly tried to impress upon me was this idea—that no matter what happened in a woman's personal life, she should never let it interfere with her medical career." According to that student, Sabin "had apparently sacrificed all of her personal social relationships for her work."[27]

Even in this extraordinary woman scientist we can see the familiar patterns common to so many others of her generation. Sabin was able to secure a fine education and an assistant's entry level job. Superior performance notwithstanding, she was promoted slowly and eliminated from the competition for the most responsible, prestigious, and powerful position in her department. She never publicly resisted unfair treatment; rather she redoubled her efforts in the hopes that superperformance would prevail. Her success may have reinforced her hope that unquestionable merit would overcome sex discrimination, but her individual success led to little protection for future female scientists.

Male researchers were not required to divest themselves of a personal life in order to qualify as dedicated scientists, although to enhance their careers they might be expected to keep their private and professional lives separate. But in the field of medical research, that most fiercely professional of medical specialties, and one that presumably required the greatest self-sacrifice for the smallest monetary rewards, women held few positions and advanced slowly. They had to prove continually that they were both dedicated and achieving.

SABIN, IN FACT, WAS THE KIND OF PERSON WHO MADE THE perfect token—emotionally undemanding and hardworking. She was particularly fortunate that her early work received considerable recognition from her mentor, Franklin Mall, and that much of her research was used by medical schools throughout the country. And upon her retirement she received the highest possible accolade from that bastion of male exclusiveness, the Harvard Medical School, which sent her a letter "con-

gratulating [her] upon a career that any man could
envy."[28]

Although apparently generous with her time and support for aspiring women, Sabin never fully recognized
that the place of female scientists was so precarious that
they could be eliminated from important professional
positions without a whisper.[29] As the only full member
at the Rockefeller Institute and the only woman directing
a laboratory, she brought two male research assistants
from Hopkins to work in her lab. She did not play a
leadership role in creating opportunities for aspiring
women, just at the time when appointments of women
were declining. Her biographer quotes her remark to a
reporter that women would gain appropriate recognition, but that "they must be prepared to work hard for
work's sake, without thought of what it may bring them
in the way of personal acclaim and emolument."[30] The
prevailing emphasis on subordination or segregation
of women scientists, and Sabin's own commitment to
superperformance as the only legitimate way to break
down barriers, were strong forces. They prevented her
from understanding that for most women individual
productivity, the creation of opportunities, and the need
for recognition could not be separated.

Some of her women colleagues had a clearer understanding of these relationships. They knew that to create
opportunities for a new generation of women called for
more than waiting for the next brilliant superperformer
to appear. When Sabin published a biography of her
mentor, a former female classmate from Hopkins wrote
to congratulate her and added: "I am hoping that now

that you are somewhat free you will take an interest as they [our professors] did in helping women to pull together and make themselves a strong force among the world's best doctors and researchists." The writer goes on to congratulate women on their success thus far. "Somewhere in your book," she told Sabin, "I saw a statement to the effect that only about five men doctors out of ten thousand were able to make a start in research. So, I think, we women made a good beginning in as much as we have you and perhaps four more." The writer did not agree with Sabin that only good work would bring more women into this select circle. "Men have always pushed men," she wrote, and added pointedly, "women are much more likely to push men than to try to bring out the best in other women."[31]

To develop a new generation of women researchers would require active participation from the most successful women, who often did not understand their crucial role in this effort. In addition, the few women at the top needed to sustain their own reputations since they were frequently being reevaluated. Even Sabin's own seemingly unassailable reputation as a scientist was revised downward as the profession began to redefine success and moved women into more marginal positions. When Sabin retired, for example, the general press and the scientific community cited her as an outstanding scientist. *Time* magazine hailed her as one of the "five keenest scientific brains in the world." Her colleagues referred to her work on the lymphatic system as one of the most significant contributions in a quarter of a century.[32] Yet subsequently, the vice president of the Rockefeller Institute, Dr. Thomas Rivers, suggested to her biographer that he believed "Dr. Sabin's greatest contribution to mankind was the work in Colorado after she retired."[33]

Was this remark simply appropriate recognition of her remarkable second career in public health when she was in her seventies? Was it actually an admission that work in public health and preventive medicine ultimately had greater impact on society than the experimental laboratory research to which Rockefeller scientists were so dedicated? Or was it an attempt to underplay her research on the lymphatic system? In this letter Rivers went on in rather guarded tones to acknowledge, "So far as I know her work on the origin of lymphatics is sound." Her research in hematology, on the other hand, "was of a controversial nature and dealt with controversial problems, some of which are still controversial."[34]

Given the state of medical research at the time, this type of controversy was not unusual. Thus by modern standards, few lasting research results can be attributed to Simon Flexner, director of the Rockefeller Institute, William Welch, dean of Johns Hopkins Medical School, or even to Sabin's colleague and mentor, Franklin Mall. Yet these men have remained legendary in the history of medical research and education. They built the departments and institutions that provided the infrastructure for modern medical research. As an investigator whose work was regularly under scrutiny, Sabin had neither the time nor the support to ensure other women's continuing success. Under the circumstances, her longevity and tireless devotion to scientific research and public service were most fortunate; had she not survived to engage in a new career in her seventies, her accomplishments at Johns Hopkins and Rockefeller might not in themselves have ensured her a lasting scientific reputation. It would be a long time before women again occupied such important positions. Opportunities to define the value of the research, to direct its course, and to select the new generation of leaders were to be privileges of power reserved for men.

Despite her later career in public health, Sabin believed that laboratory research was the most significant and prestigious kind of science. In her biographical entry for *Who's Who,* she did not even list her postretirement public health activities. Like most professionals committed to laboratory research, her priorities paralleled those of the rising research establishment.

Since medicine was primarily understood as an interventionist response to disease, pathology became the main focus of research. More specifically, leaders such as Simon Flexner looked for particular areas promising important breakthroughs that might lead to "miraculous" cures, which is why so much attention was given to tuberculosis. The failure to find a cure was a great disappointment. It was not held against Sabin particularly; but at the same time, she was the leading female researcher in this area and her lack of progress in making a breakthrough in her tuberculosis research did not win confidence for the next generation of women researchers.


FLORENCE SABIN WAS BY FAR THE MOST FAMOUS WOMAN AT the Rockefeller Institute, but a number of other women scientists held research appointments there, unlike most major universities. During its first two decades of existence (1901–1920), 180 persons were named to the scientific staff. Twenty-three of these were appointed to the most esteemed position of member (equivalent to a lifetime chair in a university).[35] Until Sabin was appointed in 1925, all members were men. Of the remaining 157 positions on the scientific staff, women were appointed to 21. In the decade between 1911 and 1920, 16.6 percent of the appointees were women, more than in all other decades in the first half century of the institute's existence. In the 1930s, by contrast, only 4 women were appointed while 165 men were added to the staff, bringing female appointments to a record low of 2.3 percent.[36]

For the twenty-six women appointed between 1901 and 1929, the length of service varied from two years to a full lifetime of service. Like the men on the staff, women holding either M.D.s or Ph.D.s worked on various research projects. Several combined their graduate study toward a Ph.D. at Columbia with research they were conducting at the institute; sometimes their degrees were awarded well into their Rockefeller tenure.

Although some of the staff members seemed to fade into obscurity, a substantial proportion of women were active professionally and centrally involved in the scientific community. Women such as Louise Pearce and Clara Lynch, who spent virtually all of their professional lives at the institute, published extensively and achieved substantial national and even international reputations. Other women went on to important positions elsewhere. Martha Wollstein became a pathologist in a pediatric hospital and an assistant professor at Columbia University; Laura Florence, a Ph.D. from Cornell, ultimately became professor of bacteriology at New York Medical College.[37]

Despite these notable successes, Rockefeller female scientists did not achieve the most prestigious appointments or the highest career rewards. Like the eminent faculty members at Mount Holyoke and other women's colleges, they were never called to Harvard, the University of Michigan, or Stanford, as their male colleagues were likely to be. These men became a pioneering group of researchers who went on to build the major science departments in the large universities. The few women in coeducational institutions taught in less prestigious schools with inferior laboratory facilities and more limited funding for research.[38] Women were rarely promoted to the top ranks. As in most colleges and universities, they were promoted much more slowly than men, received lower salaries, and were rarely awarded comparable "honors and recognition" such as invitations to join distinguished societies.[39]

Louise Pearce, for example, had one of the most distinguished careers of the female scientists at Rockefeller. In collaboration with Wade Hampton Brown, she conducted research on a variety of illnesses, including sleeping sickness, tumors, and constitutional factors of disease. The well-known Brown–Pearce tumor became standard material in experimental studies throughout the country.[40] They also developed a treatment for African sleeping sickness. Dr. Pearce went to Africa to help the colonial government in Leopoldville administer the cure. Subsequently, she received the Order of the Crown of Belgium and later was honored with the King Leopold II prize; her international reputation continued after her colleague Brown died. Yet he had been promoted to full membership at the institute, whereas she retired as an associate member.[41]

Pearce's realization that women would not be in the top decision-making positions extended beyond her research appointment. Toward the end of her career, she served as temporary president of the Women's Medical College of Pennsylvania (1946–1951). Although this job was something of a burden to one still actively engaged in research, she was hoping to open the position for a permanent appointment of a woman.[42] She was disappointed to find that her replacement was a man: "The office was put on a full-time basis with a magnificent salary and a man was appointed. The Board wanted a 'money getter' and while I do not disapprove of the chosen candidate, I still feel a woman could and should have been found. However what happened is a pure example of the same old patterns of thought and custom and I could not change it."[43]

The assumption that women were not eligible or suitable followed them throughout their careers, even as they continued to conduct research and publish papers. It was not always a conscious effort on the part of the male leadership to keep women out. Sometimes the presumption against women precluded their participation without formal rules. Margaret Rossiter, for example, has quoted a diary entry of a Rockefeller Foundation official who reviewed a committee discussion of grant applications. "Difficulties of a scientific career for a woman were discussed, and it was pointed out that while women are not officially excluded from our fellowship program, the burden of proof would be unusually heavy if such an appointment were to be made."[44]

Such a simple statement reveals the various forms of discrimination women faced in trying to build their careers. Although female applicants may never have been aware of the obstacles they faced in the fellowship process, the impact on their careers was profound. Historians of science have shown that nothing advanced scientific research in the post–World War I period as significantly as the decision of philanthropic foundations to support research scholars with postdoctorate research fellowships: "The freeing of hundreds of scientists from the routines of undergraduate teaching and academic administration during the 1920s alone was much more important to the development of science in the United States than the equipment provided by foundations, even though the latter included large telescopes and—beginning in the early 1930s—cyclotrons which were unavailable elsewhere."[45] Under such conditions the casual remark of the Rockefeller Foundation official takes on new meaning. Women's inability to compete equally for prized fellowships put them at a decided disadvantage. It impeded their research and served to reinforce the tendency to promote women slowly, and thus contributed to their marginality in the profession.

Often, women were simply not considered for important positions that might have changed the course of their careers. Alice Hamilton recounted the history of a very talented bacteriologist, Ruth Tunnicliffe, whom she knew when they were both at the Memorial Institute for Infectious Diseases in Chicago in the early 1900s. She describes Dr. Tunnicliffe as having "as brilliant success as a woman can have in that field. This means that she could be a member of any scientific society she chose, could read papers, and publish them, and win the respect of her colleagues quite as well as if she were a man, but she could not hope to gain a position of any importance in a medical school."[46]

Hamilton relates a small vignette that typified the situation many successful women scientists experienced with dreary repetition.

> I remember taking her [Tunnicliffe] to see the head of a department of pathology in a medical school where the chair of bacteriology was vacant. The pathologist received her with cordiality and respect and together they discussed their work for some time, then he spoke of the vacancy in the medical school and went over with her the qualifications of the different candidates who were being considered. Had she been a man she would almost certainly have been chosen, but it never occurred to him even to consider her.[47]

Indeed Tunnicliffe's career did not follow a trajectory to the top. She did respectable work and was the president of several local scientific societies. Although recognized in her field for her research work, she won neither a national reputation nor the opportunity for a scientific career at a major university. We can only speculate about effects of these patterns of exclusion on the character

and quality of the work of a woman who had been regarded as extraordinary in her early career.[48]

The limitations this early generation of women Ph.D.s
faced had consequences far into the future. In the first
quarter of the century women researchers in the few
prestigious places such as the Rockefeller Institute enjoyed more career mobility than women would experience again for several decades. But this encouraging beginning in a major coeducational laboratory was not to
be followed by future successes. To maintain an active
role in research institutions, women would have had to
share some of the decision-making power there. They
needed to be part of the hiring, promotion, and funding
decisions. Unfortunately, these women did not have the
opportunity to gain control of the social organization of
research. As a result, women found it almost impossible
to provide opportunities for a younger set of female colleagues that would enable them to move into research
settings, foster productivity, facilitate career mobility,
and allow them legitimate access to the top ranks.

Even those with very high professional aspirations accepted a subordinate status of assistant if it seemed necessary to gain access to research positions. Time and
again they pulled back from offering any real resistance
or challenge to the structural barriers that barred their
own advancement and hindered their ability to institutionalize opportunities for the next generation.

If we are to avoid the temptation to blame the victim,
women's restrained responses must be viewed in a larger
context. The women were few in number, their participation in decision-making positions was virtually nil,

and their political clout was minimal. All this meant that they could easily become a highly visible target for elimination, especially if their behavior were judged in the least imprudent.

Their awareness that they were unequal colleagues, included in professional settings only on the sufferance of their male superiors, conflicted with their belief in meritocracy. They wanted to believe that achieving persons would be welcomed for their abilities and contributions. Yet, they were surrounded by evidence to the contrary. In the 1920s, amid an active sense of professional organization and concern about women's rights, women's groups often did studies of inequities. Women often articulated their distress at their permanent subordination. An assistant professor of zoology observed: "I find myself apologizing for being a woman. The men who are heads of departments are so insistent upon having men, and they tell me that women ought to be satisfied to go into high schools and junior colleges. . . . During the past ten years I have stood by and helped recommend men for at least six positions that I wanted desperately badly, but being a woman I wasn't even considered."[49]

Most women were convinced that there was little use in actively resisting inequality in the workplace. Those who did not work in segregated positions believed, like Sabin, that if they pursued their research vigorously and offered continual proof of their worth, they would be recognized for their meritorious performance.

## BREAKING NEW GROUND: RESEARCH IN AN IDEALISTIC . CONTEXT

Although some women, like Sabin, internalized the values of laboratory science as completely as any of their male colleagues did, other women defined professional life differently. A strong emphasis on service ideology had emerged at the end of the nineteenth century to justify female activity outside traditional roles; at the same time, this emphasis on service legitimized the shift of essentially domestic concerns from the private to the public sphere. This was certainly the case with the settlement house workers, but it extended further. An ideology of service to the underprivileged, the young, or the sick provided the rationale for the female professions of social work, teaching, and nursing.

Scholars tend to think of scientific research as the antithesis of these "softer," more sentimental and feminine occupations. Yet there were also women whose scientific careers were informed by many of the values predominant among social workers, teachers, and socially conscious reformers. Such women scientists focused their research on the poor and disadvantaged. Concerned about issues such as birth control for poor women, lead poisoning in working men, and the quality of milk used in infants' formulas, they zeroed in on the areas that male scientists regarded as sentimental "women's work," not a worthy focus of inquiry.[50]

In reality, this kind of work often involved greater risks; researchers often found themselves in serious confrontations with employers and distributors who regarded their right to pursue a profit as sacrosanct. Even admirers of these socially conscious scientists assumed that the work involved special feminine skills. They spoke of the role women played because of their ability to combine the technical skills with "tact, persuasion, patience, intuitive imagination, rather than . . . authority."[51]

In Alice Hamilton's career we see a significant divergence from the style of Florence Sabin, though their backgrounds were not dissimilar. Sabin followed the more conventional path adopted by men—a search in immaculate laboratories for elusive solutions to biological problems. Hamilton, in contrast, created new methodologies to find solutions to concrete social problems in the fetid factories and death-dealing mines.

Hamilton's youth was spent in a conventional, well-established family in Fort Wayne, Indiana, and later at boarding school in Connecticut. After a year at an inferior local medical school in Indiana, her father agreed to send her to the University of Michigan Medical School. There she received excellent training in the new laboratory methods, especially bacteriology. Several of her professors later joined the founding faculty of Johns Hopkins. She interned at the New England Hospital for Women and Children. To further her studies in bacteriology, she went to Germany for a year, as did many who wanted to improve their research training. When she returned in 1896 no jobs were available, so she did an additional year of training at Johns Hopkins under Simon Flexner.[52] This experience brought her into the same small circle of researchers who trained Florence Sabin and Dorothy Reed—the professors who were emulating the most modern German research methods and were just embarking on the struggle to establish similar methods in a few select universities in the United States.

Hamilton's first salaried position was teaching pathology in the Women's Medical School of Northwestern University in Chicago. It was a small school, and it closed shortly after she began. She was fortunate to get an appointment in bacteriological research at the McCormick Institute for Infectious Diseases, which had recently opened. Both of these positions were in Chicago. As was the case for Anne Fearn in China, geographical location turned out to be critical to Hamilton's subsequent career, not because of immediate professional opportunities, but because she entered a new personal living situation that became crucial to her development and future career choice.

When Alice Hamilton moved to Chicago she was accepted as a resident in Hull House, the well-known settlement house headed by Jane Addams. This experience, so different from her professional socialization, was one of the most significant factors in Hamilton's career development. The settlement house brought her into daily contact with such outstanding women as Florence Kelley and Julia Lathrop. In addition, it linked her to a group of male reformers and intellectuals associated with the University of Chicago. These were the people who enlivened and articulated the political and social problems of the day. Although she went off to her work at the laboratory each day, residing at Hull House was crucial in raising Hamilton's political and social consciousness.[53]

In her first decade at Hull House she often experienced feelings of anxiety. Drawn to the active commitment of Jane Addams and other residents, Alice Hamilton often felt that by comparison her career as a scientist was not progressing satisfactorily. She described her conflicts and depression to her cousin Agnes: "I had the feeling of being pulled about and tired and yet never doing anything definite. . . . I had a bitter feeling inside that my own work was going to the winds, that I never could be a scientist."[54] She considered leaving Hull House to pursue her professional work. "I think I can do good work in science, the men I have worked for have all told me so, and if one can do good work one must, don't you think so?"[55] She ultimately decided to stay at Hull House with a more limited set of responsibilities and do some further research while studying at the University of Chicago. Slowly she began to integrate her work and private life so that each became satisfying.

Because Hull House was situated in the middle of a very poor neighborhood, Hamilton gradually developed extensive contacts with workers and their families. As a trained physician, she became acutely aware of the diseases and accidents that workers faced daily.[56] Almost nothing was known about the pervasive occupational problems omnipresent among workers. Benefits such as workman's compensation for accidents or work-related disease were still unheard of in the United States. When a group of social reformers persuaded Gov. Charles S. Deneen of Illinois to appoint a commission to survey the extent of industrial disease, Alice Hamilton was one of five physicians appointed to the commission.[57] That appointment permanently changed the direction of her work.

When the inquiry began in 1910, virtually no one understood the impact on workers of sustained exposure to lead dust, phosphorous, or mercury in the workplace. Initial investigations revealed little or no concern or knowledge on the part of employers. Hamilton was quite certain, however, that this was a major public health issue. She went on to become the leading national expert in this field, spending years accruing systematic, field-collected data and establishing statistical relationships between various chemical toxins and subsequent disease. She moved out of the laboratory and into the field. Her decision was not merely a happy accident but rather a deliberate and creative response to the biases and lacunae in establishment concerns. As she observed in her autobiographical account, the established medical professional had shown no interest in these problems and this work was unlikely to be done by men: "When I talked to my medical friends about the strange silence on this subject in American medical magazines and textbooks, I gained the impression that here was a subject tainted with Socialism or with feminine sentimentality for the poor."[58]

This type of research was distinctly different from the model of laboratory research institutionalized at the Rockefeller Institute. The line between the researchers' social-political values and the scientific questions and solutions was much more blurred. Moreover, the data and the findings were much more likely to conflict with the interests of wealthy industrialists and their socially and politically prominent supporters.[59] Thus it was more difficult for researchers such as Hamilton to maintain the disinterested posture that laboratory work permitted and encouraged.

The work was also more interdisciplinary; therefore the boundaries of professional territories and control were harder to draw. The first survey Hamilton worked on was headed by five physicians. They quickly appointed twenty assistants—doctors, medical students, and social workers—and all joined forces to organize this complex project.[60] In addition this kind of investigation was much more accessible to nonspecialists. As a result, it did not enjoy the mystique of technical language that many aspiring professionals often relied on. Industrial medical research would never lead to stunning breakthroughs, such as the discovery of antibiotics. Rather, the results would come through slow incremental empirical proofs about the consequences of breathing lead dust or handling mercury. Proposed remedies that would ameliorate the conditions of workers required costly changes in the factories. Therefore, such solutions challenged the employer's right to profit without regard to the conditions of labor. These scientific endeavors, therefore, had social consequences and risky political ramifications.

As a result of her work in Illinois, the United States commissioner of labor asked Hamilton to do a federal survey of industrial poisons. She realized that if she accepted this assignment she would never return to laboratory science. Whatever remorse she may have experienced, she modestly put aside: "I had long been convinced that it was not in me to be anything more than a fourth-rate bacteriologist."[61] Whether this would have been the case can never be known. When Hamilton made this appraisal of her own abilities as a bacteriologist, she had long been out of the center of the research network where ideas are stimulated and good research facilitated.

Instead of winning a secure position in a research laboratory, Alice Hamilton was to trek through mines and heavy war industries, breathe factory fumes, and work in urban slums in a peripatetic, courageous, and difficult career as a radical researcher. It certainly was not the kind of activity her contemporaries associated with women's work. Ironically, in later years after Hamilton became famous, many of the newspaper and magazine articles emphasized her femininity, describing her as a woman of advanced age who appeared more suited for a tea party than a lead paint factory.[62]

Hamilton herself did not miss the irony of observing life from two perspectives. In a letter to her mother in 1911 she described the steel mills of Pittsburgh.

*April 1911*

Today I went over to the West Penn Hospital to look through the records. It is an indescribably dingy place, smoke-begrimed and ugly. One of the great Carnegie Steel Mills is just below it and as I sat by the window I could watch the ambulances crawl up the hill to the accident entrance with a new victim inside. Three came while I was there. So many cases are sent from the mills that evidently the clerk got tired of writing the name of the Company and had a rubber stamp made which, appropriately enough, he uses with red ink. All down the page came these red blotches, just like drops of blood. . . .

There are queer contrasts in life, aren't there. Sunday evening I was invited to the H—'s for supper. They are in steel and very wealthy, and I was all hot inside over the luxury of the house and the complacence of Mrs. H. And then their daughter came in. She has just returned from a year at school in Italy and she is the most exquisite young thing I have ever seen, beautiful, gentle, cultivated, modest. She is the product of the ill-gotten wealth; I suppose she couldn't be so exquisite without it.[63]

Hamilton's kind of research was also subject to uncertain financial rewards and scant recognition from either the medical or the scientific professions. The new professional organizations may have emphasized raising standards, but they also gave little credence to work that did not fit their rather narrow definition of appropriate concerns, no matter what the quality of the research.[64]

Alice Hamilton rejected the profession's definition of appropriate commitments and the emphasis on value-free research. She remained concerned about political and social issues both in the work she was doing and in areas that extended far beyond her specific area of expertise. She was a member of the birth control movement and an opponent of World War I. Together with Jane Addams, a lifelong friend, she attended international peace conferences. After the war, in an atmosphere that was grossly punitive and openly hostile to anyone defined as sympathetic to the Germans, she worked actively to ameliorate the condition of starving German children.

World War I also affected her professional opportunities in ways that she had not anticipated. The breakdown of trade relations with Germany spurred the growth of domestic chemical and dye industries. When disease abounded in the plants that produced war materials, it became a subject of national concern. Some universities were then prodded into developing a new curriculum in the area of industrial medicine. Immediately after the war, Harvard University decided to make an appointment in industrial medicine. The field "still had not attracted men," Hamilton wrote, "and I was really the only candidate available."[65]

There were some among the medical school faculty who welcomed the appointment of a woman. In his letter inviting Hamilton to consider the position, the dean wrote of her unequaled qualifications for the job, and then went on to say: "Aside from my very great desire that we may be able to secure you for this work, I desire it also for the reason that I think it would be a large step forward in the proper attitude toward women in this University and in some other Universities."[66]

Hamilton was delighted with the invitation to enter the most prestigious university in the country—and the one most successful in excluding women—but she was unable to accept a full-time appointment because of her research commitments in the Labor Department. A few weeks later the dean wrote her again, inviting her to join the staff on her own terms and fill only a half-time position.[67] In the intervening weeks between his two letters,

her correspondence reveals both her enthusiasm and ambivalence about the offer and its meaning for women. To
her sister Edith she confessed: "You were dear to be so
enthusiastic about the Harvard job. But I don't believe it
is as big as Miss Thomas [Carey Thomas] said. Miss Addams thinks I ought to take it because it is important for women in general. But I can't feel that strongly
enough to take it for that reason alone. Dr. Edsall has
not yet answered my letter so it is all still in the air."[68]

When the actual invitation came two weeks later, she
sent it on to Edith with a brief postscript that expressed
both joy and apprehension: "Isn't this wonderful. Just as
I had made up my mind that I had lost my chance. . . .
Of course I have written him that I accept with joy. Only
what am I to do for six months of each year in Boston. It
appals [*sic*] me to think of it."[69]

Of course not everyone at Harvard agreed with Dean
Edsall that this appointment marked a "step forward."
President Abbott Lowell was quite explicit in stating that
her appointment must in no way be understood as opening the door to women students. The Corporation of the
University was also very upset with the medical school's
appointment: Hamilton's supporters told her later that
"one member had sworn roundly over it."[70] Those press-
ing for the appointment tried to appease the opposition.
They promised that Hamilton would never use the faculty club, nor request faculty football tickets, nor "em-
barrass the faculty by marching in the Commencement
procession and sitting on the platform."[71] If further
proof of her tokenism were needed, Harvard complied.
Hamilton was appointed as assistant professor and kept

at that rank until her retirement two decades later when she was awarded the title of emeritus.

Her arrival at the university did not go unnoticed. Newspaper reporters flocked to the scene to observe the sight of a woman lecturing. Hamilton was quick to tell reporters that "I am not the first woman who should have been appointed to the faculty of Harvard." When reporters pressed her about the question of admitting of women as students to the male bastions she at first demurred, indicating that she was unfamiliar with "the local issues involved." Speaking more generally she went on, "of course I believe in admitting women to Harvard. Isn't it the last stronghold that is now holding out against them?" Her commitment to equal education for women was profound and public. She went on to explain to the reporters: "All the other first class medical schools admit women. And if women want to make medicine their profession, surely the best school in the country should be open to them for study."[72]

Although Hamilton later wrote that she was well treated by her Harvard colleagues, she did not always find the most supportive environment in the university. In 1926 when she requested a sabbatical, she received her first positive assessment from a member of the Harvard faculty. She wrote to a friend that "He paid me the first and only compliment I have had from my faculty colleagues since I came here. He said 'well of course you're entitled to it. But whom shall we get to give your lectures? There's nobody in this country who can. We shall have to get [Edgar L.] Collis from England.' I was quite breathless with surprise, but he said it as if it were a

matter-of-course."[73] She also remained uncertain about
what her experience meant for other women; she continued to be shocked by the active hostility to women,
not only at Harvard, but also in the city of Boston,
otherwise known for its progressive movements, its
strong intellectual traditions, and generations of famous
women. Having lived in more conservative and less sophisticated places that were much more accepting of
women, she commented that "no woman can be on the
staff of any important hospital in Boston, but in New
Orleans she can." She shrewdly observed, "I think it is
the influence of Harvard, really a deeply pervading influence on the mind of Boston."[74] What she was comment-
ing on, beyond the peculiar prejudices at one university,
were the active and exclusionary practices of institutions
that also happened to be in the forefront of the march
toward professionalization.

Caught between her belief in an ideology of achievement based on merit and an environment that denigrated
and excluded professional women, it is not surprising
that she sometimes equivocated. For example, she believed women should specialize in medicine since general
practice might be exhausting. She hoped that research
might present unique opportunities for females because
"in the laboratory and in research work, a field which is
not sufficiently lucrative to hold men, women do well."[75]

In casting the issue this way, Hamilton revealed some
of the most significant assumptions held by women who
adopted creative innovation as a professional strategy.
They firmly believed in women's intellectual capability
to do first-rate work and rejected commonplace ideas

about the genetic inferiority of women. At the same time they wanted to find opportunities in new areas where they could make significant contributions without engaging in a head-on, competitive confrontation with men.

In this particular case, Hamilton guessed incorrectly. Men did not leave research to women to seek more lucrative areas of work. The power and prestige associated with defining and creating knowledge were sufficient to attract men, and they were as eager to maintain exclusivity in research positions as were the men in other specialties.

Highly successful women, like Hamilton, who had indeed reached the highest pinnacle of professional life, found it easier to see others rather than themselves as the object of prejudice. In what should be seen as a common response of successful women, she believed that she had been unusually fortunate. "I must admit that though I have seen the difficulties women doctors have to overcome, I have never suffered from them myself."[76] Her biographer pointed out that, in her autobiography, Hamilton tended to downplay the difficulties she faced in her life.[77] Part of her insistence that she was fortunate can be read as modesty. If not, how else was she to explain her ability to break down the historic barriers at Harvard? But this optimistic reading of her career sidestepped the fact that her greatest support always came from reformers and radicals who operated at some critical distance from the conventional values of society. Colleagues in the scientific professions were rarely as forthcoming in offering their endorsement.

Hamilton's devotion to her work was complemented by her membership in causes ranging from the birth control movement to the abolition of capital punishment, the defense of Sacco and Vanzetti, to her participation on Pres. Herbert Hoover's Commission on Social Trends. It was at meetings of these groups that she met other women with like interests and formed close friendships. She spent considerable time corresponding with friends—and opponents—who responded to her public positions on such controversial causes as birth control and the conviction of Sacco and Vanzetti.[78]

Hamilton's life, overall, seems particularly poignant. Her success was especially admirable since it took place in an era when the scientific profession placed substantial barriers in the path of women researchers. Her willingness to scale the redoubts of privilege and pioneer critical new areas, combining professional aspiration with political and social consciousness, resulted in great personal success. Yet, having penetrated these inner circles, she was unable to destroy the artificial barriers of prejudice that kept other women out. It was a goal that she had very much hoped to achieve. She was never able to open the doors of Harvard Medical School to women students, despite her fervent participation in the many debates on the subject.[79] Hamilton retired in 1939, and the Harvard Medical School remained closed to women until 1945.

Her general optimism about progress in American social life did not lead her to overstate the small gains that women physicians had made and the magnitude of the price they had paid. She understood even as late as 1943 that

Most people think that women in medicine have now attained equality with men but that is true in one country only, Russia. In the United States a woman finds it harder to gain entrance to the medical schools than does a man, much harder to get her internship in a first-class hospital, and difficult if not impossible to get on the staff of an important hospital. Yet without such hospital connections she can never hope to reach the highest ranks in her profession.[80]

She perceived quite clearly that women such as Sabin and herself never fully transcended the status of token. They had made their way into the institutions that exercised the most power in the profession, the very settings that were most resistant to female participation at the upper ranks. But the petty humiliations attendant on tokenism were more than amusing anecdotes to them. When Johns Hopkins passed over Florence Sabin for the position of department head, when Rockefeller subsequently downgraded her professional contribution, they were lessening the chances of success for other women. When Harvard University subjected Alice Hamilton to petty ostracisms and similarly kept her at the lowest ranks, they were, in effect, assuring that women could not have a real say in selecting and molding the future generations of professionals.

IN THE ENSUING DECADES OTHER EXCEPTIONAL WOMEN RE-searchers emerged who were also outstanding achievers. Women born a generation later than Sabin or Hamilton could occasionally be found in high-ranking places. Grace Arabel Goldsmith (1904–1975), an important researcher in medical nutrition, became the first woman dean of the School of Public Health at Tulane University, but that appointment did not occur until 1967 when she was near the age of retirement.[81] Gerty Cori (1896–1957) was the first American woman to receive the Nobel prize for medicine. But the Washington University School of Medicine prohibited faculty appointments to members of the same family, so Gerty Cori had a marginal research appointment there from 1937 on, while her husband held a regular faculty position. In 1947, the year she shared the Nobel prize with her husband and an Argentine researcher, she was finally made a full professor of biochemistry.[82] Madge T. Macklin (1893–1961), a graduate of Johns Hopkins and a pioneer in medical genetics, was never promoted beyond assistant professor, despite an international reputation and many honors.[83] The list is long and the pattern is clear. After the pioneering successes of women such as Sabin and Hamilton, a small steady stream of women had distinguished careers in medical research. Nevertheless, they were rewarded little and late, and found themselves continually pioneering new roles and proving again that women could do distinguished work.


THROUGHOUT THE TWENTIETH CENTURY ONLY A SMALL percentage of professionals, men or women, engaged in full-time research. Yet because research embodies the highest values of professional ideology, their experiences are very influential with practitioners. Researchers are often perceived as caring nothing about personal

# NEW OPPORTUNITIES IN SCIENCE

rewards; presumably they are drawn to the work only by their fascination with the possibility of solving difficult problems and finding new truths. Research, more than any other facet of professional life, is supposed to be neutral, value free, and dedicated to the betterment of humanity. We like to think it is solely an intellectual enterprise and eschews the entrepreneurial aspects of private practice. Yet if we look at the efforts to exclude and downgrade women, we can see that research is one of the most elite and exclusive areas of professional life. It is divorced from the daily routine of serving client's needs. Researchers are often engaged in working with the most specialized and least accessible ideas, which are understood by only a small group of colleagues. Research then becomes an underpinning for specialization, for the creation of a mystique of expertise that excludes not only the public, but also the vast majority of other professionals from meaningful understanding or participation, while demanding their approval and esteem because research represents the search for knowledge.[84]

It is for this reason that women's inability to re-create a second generation of researchers, who would have had access to the best laboratories and university settings, was extremely significant to subsequent generations of women. First, women could not continue to be part of the productive group of scientists who possessed a scholarly genealogy of researchers and students to continue their work. Second, only the women's colleges continued to take seriously women's professional participation in scientific research; but these institutions were limited by the fact of an undergraduate clientele as well as by financial realities. Jonathan Cole has pointed out, in his work on the history and sociology of science, that the segregation of female scientists in women's colleges essentially isolated them from interacting with many of the most able and productive men. "Thus, female Ph.D.s rarely interacted as colleagues or collaborators with the established men in their fields; they were in effect cut off from the centers of scientific and scholarly activity as a result of their job location." [85]

Sabin, Hamilton, and a few exceptional others had achieved places in these research centers, but their inability to re-create another generation of women in the rarified atmospheres of Harvard, Hopkins, or Rockefeller also meant a major setback for women in professional life. Tokenism had prevailed, and women could not confront those institutions' insistence that medical faculties could exclude them at will, that budgets would be controlled by men, that opportunities could easily be shut off by those who chose to argue that women would probably just get married anyway. [86]

Hamilton was justifiably proud of her record, but correctly dubious about its impact. "I sometimes wonder," she wrote in 1943, "whether it was not easier to make a start in the old days, when a woman doctor could count on the loyalty of a group of devoted feminists who would choose a woman because she was a woman. We do not find their like now." [87] The early women pioneers never anticipated that acceptance of a few outstanding scientists at the great universities and the major research centers as token superperformers

## NEW OPPORTUNITIES IN SCIENCE

would not be sufficient to ensure places for future generations of women. It was much easier to institutionalize
positions of laboratory technician and research assistant
where women would remain subordinate to the male
project director.

# THE CREATION
# OF PSYCHIATRIC
# SOCIAL WORK

All the women whose lives we have examined were approximately the same age. Born between 1869 and 1874, educated in the 1890s in the new graduate programs, they were part of the generation that assumed their initial professional positions at the turn of the century. It was just at this time that universities were asserting new standards, and the professions were actively touting the accomplishments of their newly trained M.D.s and Ph.D.s.

In the wake of these successes, other occupations began earnest efforts to develop graduate programs. They also established licensing procedures and professional structures that would enhance their control over certain services. Psychiatric social work was one such field. Although there had been attempts to initiate social work programs from the 1890s on, the initial courses did not offer degrees. Their early emphasis was on training volunteers, and there was little agreement in the field about what the curriculum should be. Some envisioned a field that would focus on political organizing and public policy—working for child labor laws, improving municipal services, and generating other state actions to improve the lives of the poor. Others thought that the main occupational focus should be on medical social work—assisting families of patients and providing doctors with additional knowledge about home conditions that might

# CREATION OF PSYCHIATRIC SOCIAL WORK

contribute to illness. Efforts to develop psychiatric social work education as a special subfield did not occur
until the end of World War I.[1]

The two women who are the central figures of this
chapter, Mary C. Jarrett and Bertha C. Reynolds, were
both connected to the Smith College School for Social
Work. Both a decade or more years younger than professionals such as Reed or Hamilton, Neilson, or Putnam
in other fields. But the pioneering efforts of the psychiatric social workers were no less dramatic than those of
earlier figures in medicine, science, or college teaching.
Attempting to gain access to new professional opportunities, these women were endlessly resourceful. Sabin,
Reed, and others managed to penetrate the traditional
professions controlled by men; by contrast, these social
work pioneers built a new female profession. In psychiatric social work we observe a telling example of
women using a strategy of innovation to create new
opportunities.

Social work, a profession founded by women for
women, drew on the historical tradition of women's volunteer work in aiding the poor as "friendly visitors." To
that tradition it added the determined efforts for assisting the poor that had been developed by a generation of
college graduates in the settlement houses in all the
major cities. In creating psychiatric social work, the
founders were seeking to convert the traditions of charity
and reform into paid professional work and to use psychology and psychiatry as the intellectual core of the
field. These pioneers believed that advanced education
and the development of a psychiatric casework method

would provide the trainees with scientific training. This was no easy task, and it required a firm and self-conscious commitment to emerging professional patterns.

Their goals and activities eventually produced an attractive opportunity for graduate study in a new field that would be largely occupied by women. And if the idea of graduate school seemed ambitious compared with the previous charitable practices, it fit with the emerging conceptions of other professional fields on which psychiatric social work was modeled. The call for scientific training, the insistence on merit for membership in the profession, as well as the orientation toward service were all consonant with the claims of the traditional professions; the psychiatric social workers were simply moving in the same direction as the other fields.

However, two differences were apparent. First, the women were aware that they were trying to create a new specialty in a field where the early commitments to service had been centered on the poor and needy—groups that the other professions avoided. Now their purpose was to upgrade their training and make good their claim to work alongside male professionals, without competing with the men's areas of expertise. Second, because the majority of the social work professionals were women, the field followed a different course of development. Despite their best efforts, the founders soon realized that female social workers would not achieve the autonomy, the power, or the prestige that the psychiatrists they worked with would claim for themselves.

This inability to achieve equal professional status and rewards had roots in both the psychiatric social workers'

training and in their field experience. The structure of academe in the early twentieth century was predominantly male controlled, especially at the graduate levels. Ordinarily the deans or directors of the social work schools were men who held Ph.D.s, as they were at the Smith College School for Social Work. In the field, the practicing graduates were ordinarily supervised by male M.D.s and psychiatrists, even though the predominant numbers among the social work practitioners were always women. Psychiatric social workers were never successful in challenging or changing these power relationships; as a result they never achieved the kind of internal autonomy, control of membership, and prestige that their models, the physicians, were able to garner for themselves. As a consequence, from their inception the social workers were concerned with status problems, always wondering if they were truly professionals.[2]

Of course structural inequality of the type we are describing could barely have been understood by contemporaries in an emerging field. Given the milieu in which social work was created, its subsequent difficulties as a profession would have been difficult for anyone to have anticipated. These new schools initiated new occupations for educated women that would not compete directly with established male fields. Social work benefited not only professional women, but also offered social amelioration for the powerless and the needy through the attractive possibilities that modern expertise appeared to

Opposite: Mary C. Jarrett. Courtesy of Smith College Archives.

offer. But despite their staunch commitments to the model established in several fields, the status of social work remained in doubt for reasons that become clearer as we examine the Smith School in more detail.

The Smith College School for Social Work was one of more than a dozen schools of social work founded in this period. It led the field in developing an exclusive focus on psychiatric social work and was, by all accounts, a successful experiment. Mary C. Jarrett was the original founder. A graduate of Goucher College, she received most of her social work training as an apprentice to a psychiatrist in Boston, Dr. E. E. Southard. Together they pioneered the clinical approach that became the hallmark of psychiatric social work and coauthored a book on psychiatric problems, *The Kingdom of Evils: 100 Case Histories*. After organizing a summer institute to train social workers at Smith College in 1918, Jarrett was instrumental in establishing a permanent graduate program. She became the associate director of the new school and remained there until 1923.[3]

Bertha C. Reynolds, one of Jarrett's original students at the first Smith training program, was the associate director of the Smith College School for Social Work in 1925–1938. Although one of the first students of psychiatric social work, Reynolds went on to become a maverick in the field. In the latter part of her career she moved

Opposite: Bertha C. Reynolds, 1938. Bertha Reynolds Papers. Courtesy of Stoughton Historical Society and Sophia Smith Collection, Women's History Archive, Smith College.

from an exclusive interest in psychoanalytic theory to an increasing attraction to Marxism and the radical organizing efforts of the 1930s. She never abandoned her hope of developing a synthesis between her interest in individual pathology and her commitment to a structural analysis of poverty and social deviance.[4] Neither Jarrett nor Reynolds ever earned a degree in social work: all their training came from short-term institutes or on the job. Yet they were dedicated to establishing the rigorous graduate programs that would propel the field forward in its efforts to assert professional claims.

The leaders of the movement expected no argument when they insisted that scientific training was a necessary component of professional work and that access to the profession should be limited to the most qualified.[5] No longer were leisure and the desire to do good sufficient qualifications for serving the poor. The Smith School founders were clear that the newly emerging fields of personality development and psychology must serve as the cognitive core of professional social work, thus separating themselves even further from the old friendly visitor tradition and aligning themselves with psychiatrists and psychologists. They were sensitive to the criticisms that social work had no intellectual focus and thus did not enjoy professional status.

The effort to create a profession of social work had few antecedents on which to build. Even scientific research, a brand new field in 1900, modeled itself on the German example. The women and men who were committed to developing social work had the successful examples of medicine, law, and science. Yet while they wanted parity with other professionals, they were struggling to distinguish social work from other allied fields. To understand this early groping for professional definition and its impact on later developments, let us look first at an attempt to define the field at its inception.

## THE DIAGNOSIS OF THE OUTSIDE EXPERT

As early as 1915, several years before the opening of the Smith College School for Social Work, the National Conference on Charities and Corrections, which subsequently became the National Association of Social Work, asked the influential educator Abraham Flexner to deliver a paper on social work at their annual meeting. Significantly, he chose as his topic, "Is Social Work a Profession?" His challenging analysis of social work posed questions about its professional status that the social work leaders considered crucial.[6] As far as his contemporaries were concerned, Flexner's previous work on the medical profession, and his Ph.D., made him one of the leading authorities in the nation on the subject of professionalism.[7] The set of assumptions and the value laden assessment that Flexner provided for his audience was subsequently absorbed by the emerging social work profession as part of its self-definition and helped to determine its professional goals.

Flexner found problematic the questions of the exact professional nature of social work. He argued that the social worker's professional pretensions were jeopardized by the need for "collaboration" with other professionals. Further, the goals of social work made it "not so much a definite field as an aspect of work in many fields." He also observed, with what must have been some measure of fortitude since this paper was offered at the National Conference on Charities and Corrections, that "the width of scope characteristic of social work" necessarily led to "a certain superficiality of attainment, a certain lack of practical ability," although he gallantly added that this should not be "a matter for reproach."[8]

Flexner was concerned in those early years about social work's lack of intellectual rigor and disciplinary focus. He observed that "it may be that social work will gain if it becomes uncomfortably conscious that it is not a profession in the sense in which medicine and engineering are professions; that if medicine and engineering have cause to proceed with critical care, social work has even more."[9]

After this devastating critique he changed gears at the end of the paper and assured his audience that "after all, what matters most is professional spirit." He observed that all activities may be prosecuted (even presumably social work) in the genuine "professional spirit." In the last analysis "the unselfish devotion of those who have chosen to give themselves to making the world a fitter place to live in can fill social work with the professional spirit and thus to some extent lift it above all the distinctions which I have been at such pains to make."[10]

Flexner was accurate in fastening on the need for a cognitive center; establishing an area of expertise was a crucial step in professionalization. But social work was not alone in facing this problem. It is also true that other professions in 1915, when he gave this address, could barely verify clear disciplinary boundaries of a scientific nature. In fact, only five years earlier, in the 1910 report on the medical profession, his great contribution had been to recommend revisions of the woefully inadequate curricula in all but a handful of medical schools.[11]

What the traditional professions, such as medicine and law, had in common that social work lacked was a tradition of paid work and a predominance of male practitioners who could draw on reservoirs of power in the larger society, that their gender and social status conferred on them.[12] Even the new professions such as scientific research were able to claim associations with the most powerful universities in the country and lavish foundation funding. Implicit in Flexner's examples, and probably quite unconscious, was his unstated criterion that indisputable claim to professional status required that the majority of the practitioners be men. At one point in his speech the patriarchal underpinnings of the discussion became almost palpable, when he observed that

> a profession is a brotherhood—almost, if the word could be purified of its invidious implications, a caste. Professional activities are so definite, so absorbing in interest, so rich in duties and responsibilities, that they completely engage their votaries. The social and personal lives of professional men and their families thus tend to organize around a professional nucleus. A strong class consciousness soon develops.[13]

In this light, Flexner's final invocation of "professional spirit" as "unselfish devotion" contained a double

irony for the women professionals in his audience. Unselfish devotion, as an expression of truly professional
behavior, would require them to forego marriage, for
only "professional men" could reasonably expect that
their "social and personal lives" and that of their families
would "organize around" their professional needs. There
is an additional irony in prescribing the requirements for
professional goals and equality to women social workers
while excluding their members, by definition, from the
"brotherhood." In the end one could interpret that speech
as a call to direct the aims of the social workers to do
their share in a vaguely defined attempt to "make the
world a fitter place to live in,"[14] without trying to resolve the questions of power and status for social work's
practitioners.

## DEVELOPING A GRADUATE CURRICULUM

The early history of the Smith College School for Social
Work reflected concern for the professional status questions raised by Flexner. Even before the school opened,
the founders understood that they had to address the
question of appropriate work and training for women as
well as Flexner's concerns about intellectual rigor and a
cognitive center. Mary Jarrett was particularly sensitive
to the needs of the new field she hoped to have a hand in
developing.

Jarrett, who encompassed in her own lifetime this
move from charity worker to paid professional, was born
in 1877 in Baltimore. After graduating from Woman's

College of Baltimore (later Goucher College) in 1900, she did some volunteer work for the Baltimore Charity Organization. From this typical female activity, she moved to a paid position and the beginning of a lifetime career in social work and social work education.[15]

In 1903 Jarrett took a position as welfare worker with the Children's Aid Society where she was trained on the job in the emerging casework method. These early casework positions placed great emphasis on attention to individuals' needs, but did not incorporate any ideas about psychology or psychiatry. By the time she left a decade later, she was the head of the casework department. For the next four years Jarrett worked at the Boston Psychiatric Hospital, where its influential director, Dr. E. F. Southard, invited her to organize and head a social service department.[16] Her collaboration with Southard was a turning point for her because together they developed the clinical team approach to patients with psychiatric disorders—which they named psychiatric social work. They were interested in applying this method of working with patients to a broad range of society and actively sought support for studies of psychiatric problems in industry. The field was essentially unformed. It took them several years to persuade the Engineering Foundation to support a study to investigate psychiatric disorders in workers, with the hope of developing counseling and rehabilitation options for engineers with psychological problems.[17]

Jarrett became increasingly convinced that there were real possibilities for career development in the field of psychiatric social work. As the United States became involved in World War I, she developed courses for social welfare workers who were working with soldiers at the hospital. In 1918, with Southard's encouragement, she transferred this activity to Smith College where she developed an intensive summer training program for psychiatric social workers.

The opportunity to develop such a course had several purposes. First, Southard and Jarrett were interested in moving the field away from preoccupation with the poorest groups in the society. They thought that the soldiers' reactions to stress were parallel to civilian's responses to high-stress situations. Thus, understanding the relationship between emotions and certain symptoms should have wide applicability.[18] Beyond this, they believed that the sociologists who had been instrumental in the early phases of social work had started some of the schools of social work off on the wrong track. Southard and Jarrett were determined to teach their students to individualize each person instead of emphasizing classes of people, such as the poor, the elderly, or the abused.[19]

There was a sense of excitement in Jarrett's first class at Smith. Women of all ages, most from New York, Philadelphia, Boston, and Baltimore, and a few from places as distant as Wisconsin, congregated in Northampton. Many were looking for a way to participate in the war effort when this opportunity arose. A number of famous psychiatrists gave guest lectures, and the forty women felt as if they were on the cutting edge of a new field.[20] Neither Southard nor Jarrett were Freudians; they were of a more empirical bent and believed the analysts could not prove any of their findings scientifically. But they knew that Freud and his followers were developing theories that were considered important, and they made sure that their students were conversant with these new ideas.[21]

Southard was pleased and delighted with the Smith School experiment and expressed surprise that his idea "would come so quickly to fruition."[22] The National Committee for Mental Hygiene, spurred on by Southard's work in psychiatric training, appointed a subcommittee that cooperated with various private and public institutions and the Boston State Hospital trustees to work with Smith College to set up a program.[23]

Despite this excellent response, some reservations were voiced. The initial evaluation of the first summer institute reflected the special problems of creating a profession especially attractive to women. Comments ranged from the trivial—would Northampton's summer prove to be too much of an obstacle for women to engage in serious study—to the more serious problem of convincing the public that women had the intellectual and personal capacities to delve into the mysteries of the psyche.[24] Dorothy Reed had to stay on a hospital ward in Baltimore all summer to prove she was better than her fellow medical students. In social work the problem took a different form. The whole profession had to adopt a demeanor that did not threaten men but still gave evidence of professional rigor.

To address this issue Smith's president, William A. Neilson, underlined the argument of service, the mainstay of many who supported higher education for women. Useful female employment would emphasize service rather than success. But clearly this was not

enough to justify and support the development of a professional curriculum. Southard, who profoundly supported women's entrance into this new field, was sensitive
to the need to justify offering the "somewhat strong food
of modern psychiatry and psychopathology" to women.
In his view the problem had two dimensions; one had to
do with what "publicities were permissable," which
probably should be understood to mean what could
properly be said aloud. The other was the almost equally
delicate question of women's capacity to learn. Southard
understood that "there could not be a branch of psychiatric social work for women if women could not understand (and so to say metabolize) the main psychiatric
facts as they affect society." [25] Fortunately he was able to
assure those who had doubts that women "were able to
get the main facts of social psychiatry without a trace of
evil reaction or discomfort." By way of further reassurance, Southard pushed his case and observed that
"these women get a fuller account of the general aspects
of mental diseases than medical students in their third
year ordinarily get in medical schools." He was then obli-
ged to backtrack somewhat and add parenthetically that
"of course, I do not mean to insist that what they got,
though in some sense fuller, was in any sense an equivalent of medical instruction." [26] A female-dominated new
profession could never claim to be the equal of the rapidly ascending medical profession.

Jarrett and Southard were determined to develop a
new curriculum based on casework. But their casework
would go beyond what earlier social work educators had
called for. They believed that personality development

was the key to providing casework with a cognitive center and had great hopes for the new mental hygiene movement. This new disciplinary focus of psychiatric social work held out both promise and problems for the aspiring professionals. On the one hand, it seemed to offer a new area of training, not yet monopolized by more powerful professions and not as easily open to the untrained "friendly visitors." It could provide a certain mystique that helped justify the professional's role. It also held out really radical possibilities for a new understanding of human behavior—substituting an understanding of the psyche for older ideas about moral deficiencies. On the other hand, it was an approach that, at best, was just emerging; therefore it was very difficult to subject to empirical testing.[27]

Jarrett's relationship with Southard was crucial. He had trained her and given her an opportunity to develop these new methods. She had enormous admiration for him. She knew he had wanted someone to help him implement some of his new ideas and that he had picked her because she was bright and alert, had excellent administrative ability, and good control of her emotions.[28] She respected his intelligence and warmth and genuine commitment to the development of this field.

Southard also provided her with the necessary professional legitimacy, which helped compensate for her lack of advanced degrees. In 1919 the new training school at Smith was established. The application form gained additional significance for the school because it was sponsored by the National Committee for Mental Hygiene and also because it was signed by a roster of physicians headed by Southard.[29] But it was Jarrett who actually went to Northampton to establish the program. She was the person with experience in social work and clearly the most important person at the school. Still, she was not allowed to serve as director because she did not have the necessary credentials. Given the assumptions concerning the nature of professionalism and its focus on credentials, this must have seemed a reasonable decision in an academic setting, despite the fact that there were no advanced degrees in social work and that she had worked closely with Southard and was certainly qualified in terms of experience. In 1919 F. Stuart Chapin was appointed as director, and Jarrett became the associate director.[30] Chapin was professor of sociology at Smith College and could offer the prestige of a Ph.D. to the office.

As associate director Jarrett was a leading force at the school in developing a curriculum and institutionalizing a professional training program. She saw her task in several ways. First, she wanted to develop a set of transferable casework skills, which many people still did not believe possible. With the encouragement of Southard and Chapin, she built the foundation for a psychiatric casework curriculum, in spite of the skepticism of many critics in the field.

The war ended soon after the first class finished their training, so they never had a chance to work with soldiers as they had planned. Instead, they went to work in family agencies or with the Red Cross. In these settings they felt their psychiatric social work training was valuable and no longer defined it as a special war-related skill. Because they wanted some ongoing forum to meet and talk about their experiences, many thought of joining a local chapter of Hospital Social Workers. But the hospital workers seemed too far removed from the concerns of the social workers trying out their new psychiatric casework skills. So Jarrett, together with her friend Maida Solomon, organized the Psychiatric Social Workers Club. They began to spread their ideas across the country, and the club eventually became the psychiatric section of the National Association of Social Workers.[31] This was one more sign that psychiatric social workers separated themselves from other branches of the field—and feelings were not always friendly between the groups.

Jarrett wrote, lectured, and actively lobbied for the development of a career that combined knowledge of psychiatry with the more conventional social work tasks of working with the families of patients in the hope of manipulating the social environment. In one article in a series on careers for women, she wrote: "In all forms of social work there is need of knowledge of psychiatry and the psychiatric point of view (to look for mental cases of conduct and for individual differences) since about 50 per cent of all social cases are psychiatric problems (involving persons in some degree or other of psychopathic behavior) and since mind is an important factor in all efforts for social adjustment."[32]

This radical view of social problems, which looked to the new growing interest in psychiatry, put Jarrett somewhat at odds with Mary Richmond, who was the acknowledged leader of the field of social work education and who was not very interested in psychiatric or psychological ideas.[33] When Richmond's book, *Social Diagnosis,* was published, Jarrett gave it a critical review. Despite the lack of enthusiasm from some leaders and some personal animosity toward Mary Jarrett, the New York School of Social Work and the Pennsylvania School of Social Service soon joined Smith in offering psychiatric social work programs as jobs became available.

"The mental hygiene movement [as they began to call the mental health field] has grown so fast," Jarrett wrote, "that there are ten jobs for every worker in clinics, hospitals, reformatories, the Red Cross and even in the courts."[34] She hoped that the list of places of employment would expand to include industry. She encouraged women to think about this career with its ample opportunities and its salaries ranging from $1,200 to $2,000, amounts that exceeded the salaries of most teachers. Jarrett was specific about the necessary qualifications for the new career: "One needs a natural fitness to work with disturbed people, an education equivalent to college, professional training in social psychiatry, and a practicum or supervised internship."[35] This kind of training would center on objective observation and knowledge of personality development and mental disorders and would reject the moralistic voice that so often accompanied the unprofessional friendly visitor.

The growing development of the field caused some dissension. While Jarrett and her colleagues saw the mental hygiene movement opening new worlds, others in the field believed the focus on personality disorder would turn attention away from social problems, making the profession more conservative than it had been at the turn of the century.

Just as Jarrett's career seemed to be reaching its zenith, she lost her position at Smith College School for Social Work. Southard had died and Chapin had been replaced as director by Everett Kimball, professor of history and government, who had been a member of the Smith faculty since 1904. He had no particular training in social work, but he did have the advantage of a Ph.D. from Harvard. Jarrett did not get along with Kimball, and in 1922 she felt compelled to resign. She was bitterly disappointed and never fully understood what had happened to exclude her.[36] In part, she was the victim of the rising professional standards at the women's colleges. As a tireless worker for the development of a graduate program, she herself had no graduate degrees. Stuart Chapin, the first director of the Smith School, who had left for the University of Minnesota, tried to console her by suggesting that

> I think the Smith situation can be explained by the fact that the faculty is dominated by an influential group of scholars with a narrow classical slant and that any appointment that does not carry traditional graduate degrees, especially if it is an appointment that seems to recognize any practical subject, is opposed and cried down. This is what you were up against. It was largely for this reason that I was glad to accept this position with its freedom and great opportunities, and get away from a cramped atmosphere.[37]

Kimball himself also told Jarrett subsequent to her resignation that he had wanted an associate director who could be a member of the faculty and that such an appointment required graduate degrees. Others suggested that some of the Smith alumnae thought that the associate director should be a Smith graduate.[38] But Jarrett herself sensed that this growing emphasis on degrees was not the whole story. In her own handwriting she noted on Chapin's letter to her that the "School still has an Associate Director with no graduate degree. So there is more to it."[39]

In fact there was more to it. Soon after Kimball had been appointed, the school asked an influential group of Smith alumnae, working in the field of social services, to review the direction of the social work program, and especially to consider its future potential as a full-fledged graduate school. The committee, headed by Mary van Kleeck, the distinguished social researcher and reformer, developed a very critical assessment of Mary Jarrett and her role at the school. Several committee members believed that the supervision of untrained students working in social agencies was poor and that a full-time supervisor should be appointed to replace Jarrett. But their criticisms went further; they made it clear to Kimball that Jarrett did not have their crucial support to continue at Smith. "Why," wrote one member of the committee, "do the girls coming from the Smith Training School think they are so much better than anyone else? . . . I am sure," she insisted, "the Associate Director has instilled that into them quite firmly."[40] Another alumna wrote Kimball about a Smith student working in her agency in Chicago. She described in some detail her views of this timid student's difficulties in the agency. She then went on to say that this poor student had confided to her that she was afraid to go back to Smith because she had a terrible problem with Miss Jarrett, whom she described as a very poor teacher. The letter goes on to report to Kimball that Ida Cannon, a well-known social work pioneer at Massachusetts General Hospital, had little regard for Jarrett.[41] Kimball responded by saying that he needed some time to change the leadership at the school, but that he understood the situation and basically concurred with their assessment. He thought it politically unwise to dismiss her summarily at the behest of alumnae, but rather hoped the situation would develop in such a way that she would resign of her own accord.[42]

In trying to interpret this conflict that led to the ouster of Jarrett, there is, of course, the question of individual personality and fit. Was Jarrett deficient as associate director? Had she become difficult when she took over this second-in-command position? Students in the early classes remembered her as a highly professional, occasionally intimidating person who distanced herself socially from other people. Yet they believed that she had great knowledge and conviction and was always teaching—both in class and out.[43]

Jarrett knew she was treading on dangerous ground as she trained the first psychiatric social workers. She continually urged them to be careful about flaunting their knowledge in front of psychiatrists or clients. One early student recalled: "Miss Jarrett gave us sound advice, never to mention certain mechanisms in the presence of psychiatrists, because that amounted to threatening their professional stature. It looked to them like boasting. We didn't always follow that advice, but we always treated it respectfully. I guess our natural timidity helped out."[44]

## CREATION OF PSYCHIATRIC SOCIAL WORK

Another alumna of the first class had a similar recollection about modesty and caution: "She had told us here at Smith that many of these sophisticated ideas you can't use in public. You can't be too frank with your clients, because they'll wonder why you ladies who look so much like ladies know so much. If you haven't experienced it, how could you get it all from books? So, in order to prevent that reputation, you better learn to keep it quiet for a while until it's better known. And, so we learned, ourselves, that had to be so."[45]

Despite her sensitivities to the possibility of offending physicians or the public, she underestimated the power of the rivalries among different types of social workers. True, her main critics were Smith alumnae who may not have welcomed an outsider, but this was also the group of individuals identified with Massachusetts General Hospital (a rival to Boston Psychopathic in attempting to carve out medical social work under the leadership of Richard Cabot and Ida Cannon). Then there was Russell Sage, where Mary van Kleeck and her colleagues developed an investigation of women's working conditions in New York City, and there were still other critics among the Visiting Nurses Association. All these groups were in competition with the new psychiatric social workers who were so filled with the possibilities of their new-found expertise. Jarrett's cool, aloof manner probably did not help persuade them of the legitimacy of her vision, and her students' sense that they were part of the formation of a new field might easily have been interpreted as arrogance on the part of those who believed in a different style of social work.[46]

The situation was made even worse because Jarrett was closely identified with Southard, whose own prestige waned at this time, when Freudian ideas began to replace earlier psychiatric typologies of the kind that Southard had pioneered. Since she was not part of the elite Smith alumnae network, Jarrett could never count on their support for her continued leadership at Smith College's new graduate school, even though she had been so instrumental in starting it.[47] Her friend Maida Herman Solomon understood this. She thought that with the death of Southard, Jarrett had lost her mentor and protector.

> I believe that one acts differently when one has a leader in the movement as next friend and particularly as fearless and tactless as Dr. S. was. He didn't hesitate to make enemies and you went along with him in a sort of intellectual honesty and insistence on your standards, principles, and methods. So your enemies were his—May Kline, etc. and you were swept out of the Psycho (Boston Psychopathic Hospital) on that wave. Then I think you acted the same way on your own with Kimball—instead of compromising—being tactful or what not.[48]

Solomon goes on to caution Jarrett not to get involved in any further conflict. "I think the impression in Boston is rather firmly fixed that you are difficult." Instead Solomon counseled her to stand on her record and demonstrate that the curriculum structure she laid down at Smith and at Boston Psychopathic Hospital was the one being adopted at other institutions with little change or improvement.[49]

This kind of response must have been very difficult for Jarrett, who clearly sought approval and felt under-appreciated for her contributions. It was not easy for her to put the situation to rest. She notes on the letter that she was not responsible for the break with Kimball: "For a winter and two summers I accommodated myself to Mr. Kimball but didn't want to continue. This was not the actual difficulty. Kimball was jealous and resented any attention I received. He was a petty man and I came to dislike him." [50]

Petty or not, Kimball remained the director for over two decades, and Mary Jarrett, the founder of the school, had to look for a new position. She was offered several possibilities in Chicago, but not in psychiatric social work education. Some urged her to continue, even if the circumstances were not ideal, in order to show the possibilities of psychiatric social work as a career:

> It would help your prestige, I think, to come out here. I know that you don't care much for this, but I think you have a duty toward the work. You know well that there are very few well-trained psychiatric social workers. You know also that you are the leader in this field and that you are so regarded by everyone. You will not be doing your full duty by psychiatric social work or by your own abilities, it seems to me, by either leaving the field or by taking a subordinate or relatively unimportant part in the work. [51]

But Jarrett did leave the field. She and her lifetime companion, Katrine Collins, moved to New York City where Mary Jarrett spent the rest of her career working on programs for the chronically ill. [52]

As a founder and leader she was successful in developing a curriculum that had a profound impact on social work education. As a woman without full professional credentials she found herself dependent on the good will of the men who were better placed. When those connections were severed and she did not have a strong female network to replace them, she lost the capacity to develop a full career in the world of psychiatric social work.

This pattern of leadership remained set at the Smith School and was often replicated in many places throughout the country. Typically, the director was a man. He had the faculty connections and the administrative authority. He depended on his female associate director, who had much more actual experience with clients and social agencies, to provide the daily connections between students and the social agencies; in addition, he wanted a supportive relationship with his associate. In short, too much independence on the part of the associate director was not acceptable. She needed the protection of a strong male figure or, at a minimum, a politically powerful female network.

## THE NEXT STAGE

Two years after Mary Jarrett left Smith, Bertha Reynolds became the associate director. Reynolds had been born in 1885 to a problem-laden family. Her father died when she was very young, and her mother often seemed overwhelmed by the obligations of raising a family on very limited funds. An aunt who ran a preparatory school in Northampton made it possible for her to prepare for and attend Smith College from 1904 to 1908. Reynolds had a difficult adolescence; she was shy and unable to develop a much-desired social life. After graduation she went through a stormy period. She began teaching and then had a "nervous breakdown" as she termed her bout with depression and anxiety that sent her home to her family. As she recovered, she decided to turn to social service and took a one-year course at Simmons College that enabled her to get a job at Boston Children's Aid Society. Her growing interest in psychology led her in 1918 to enroll as a student in the first summer training program in psychiatric social work at Smith College, where she came to know and respect the work of Mary Jarrett and E. E. Southard.[53]

Reynolds took her newly developed casework skills to Danvers State Hospital where she became the director of social services. At Smith she had learned to read and admire Freud and to develop ideas about psychological development and psychiatric disorders. She also remembered the practical advice Mary Jarrett had given the students: "I found I could use a great deal. We were warned not to talk about psychoanalysis before a psychiatrist unless very tentatively and very modestly."[54] This helped her maintain harmonious relations with the physicians with whom she worked. It did not, however, help social workers develop professional authority when they had to hide their expertise.

Despite some satisfaction with her work, Reynolds continued to feel personally inadequate. Unlike many women professionals, who deliberately chose not to marry, she was disappointed by her failure to develop a serious relationship with a man.

It is incredible, I know, to anyone reared since World War I that a woman who really wanted marriage could not do anything to attain at least a few friends of the other sex. No one who has not lived in them could believe how powerful were the taboos against any female initiative in which I was reared. . . . I felt hopelessly handicapped without good looks or conversational graces, and with too much intellectual capacity (which I had never wanted and tried to deny) which I knew men *didn't want* in a woman.[55]

Reynolds was about fifteen years younger than Nellie Neilson, Bertha Putnam, or Alice Hamilton; no doubt this age difference in part affected Reynolds's attitude toward marriage. She came to maturity in an age when marriage rates were rising, and she felt the powerful pull of family life, although she believed she had little opportunity to fulfill her dream. The field of social work was much more ill formed than that of medicine or research, and initially it was harder for Reynolds to find a strong group of like-minded women. At Mount Holyoke or in the settlement houses, women had developed a thriving subculture. They commonly paired up in living arrangements and developed an integrated social and professional life. In Boston, Reynolds keenly felt the lack of such supports and the constraints of a rigid society. She wrote: "Single women were just beginning to have apartments then, but as late as BCAS [Boston Children's Aid Society] days [1910s] when two staff girls pooled their funds and hired a 'tenement' to live in they were whispered about as possibly homosexual."[56] Amidst all these constraints, she felt very lonely and began to turn more and more to her work for satisfaction.

In 1925 Reynolds unexpectedly received an urgent call from Everett Kimball asking her to become associate director of the Smith College School for Social Work. With no advanced degree (neither the course at Simmons nor the program she took at Smith offered an M.A. when she had attended) and no preparation in sociology, she felt very unprepared. In addition she had grave misgivings about her personal suitability for mixing with such cultured people.

Kimball prevailed upon her and was able to assuage her doubts. She was flattered and excited and finally accepted. She later reflected: "I think now that EK's persuasive disposing of all my objections was due to his personal need to have somebody with whom he could get along as associate director. He had emerged rather battered from three years with two who did not get on with him. . . Later people told me that the Smith School was so unpopular that it would have gone on the rocks unless someone could be found to improve its relations with agencies in the field."[57]

Reynolds was forty years old when she went to Smith to take on this new role. She thrived in this atmosphere, enjoying a supportive and developing relationship with Kimball in the first years. He depended on her knowledge of the field and her ability to develop good ties with the agencies in which their students had placements.

She ultimately became an effective teacher and developed a reputation as an educational maverick. She rejected the traditional pedagogy that students were accustomed to and substituted discussion classes for lectures and rote memory. As part of her own education she slowly became acclimated to the "liberated" atmosphere of the twenties, even recovering from her initial shock at seeing women students smoke and drink at parties.

Her increasing immersion in the burgeoning field of psychiatry did not blind her to the dangers of adopting this approach uncritically. She observed with some discomfort that the attempt to convert the older charity workers to professionals was not always successful. These former volunteers often carried old social attitudes with them that were not always in the clients' best interests: "The older women who had come to learn 'the psychiatric approach' by which to dominate their clients more tactfully, and hence more successfully, were baffling." [58]

Since the Smith program was concentrated in the summers, faculty used the winters to work in agencies and to monitor students in the field. This gave Reynolds the opportunity to travel and do research in social agencies. In this way she became increasingly well known in the field. At the same time she began to be concerned about the tendency of social workers to attribute all problems to psychological causes. From 1927 to 1932, for example, she worked winters in the Institute for Child Guidance in New York, a lavishly funded place that was to be a "show case" training institute for psychiatrists, psychologists, and social workers in the rapidly growing field of child development. Looking back on the situation at a later period in her life, she reflected: "We were blinded (as we had to be in a venture supported by big money) to the effect of low wages, poverty, race discrimination and the like, and saw only the failure of parents with their children. We succeeded too often in making parents feel that *they* had no alibi." [59]

These concerns were only intermittently distressing during the twenties but surfaced as a major crisis in social work during the depression of the 1930s. Reynolds found herself sympathetic to social workers in the field who were forced to administer relief funds in ways that they often believed were destructive to the clients they were trying to benefit. Some younger workers actively supported the development of unemployed councils and other political groups. Others began to organize to defend their own rights as public assistance workers or employees of private federations; these social workers decided to make their concerns about standards of practice public. Reynolds supported these activist social workers who demonstrated, passed out leaflets, and employed other standard organizing practices.[60]

The tension between psychiatric social work and community organizing had been present in social work from the beginning. But by the thirties psychiatric social work was the more conservative approach—emphasizing intrapsychic problems rather than social factors as causes of family breakdown, alcoholism, or the myriad other problems their clients faced. As group work or community organizing became associated with radical political activity, it became even more threatening to leaders in the field and to their funders.

Reynolds was one of the few older people to support the young organizers. She defined their efforts as a logical response to the situation and saw her own involvement as an extension of her teaching. She became a member of the advisory board of a new radical journal, spoke publicly in professional forums on behalf of labor organizing efforts, and was increasingly identified with left-wing causes.[61] She later observed: "These [methods of demonstrating] were characterized by comfortable leaders in social work as crude, vulgar, and adolescent, but they got results in increasing public awareness of the bitter needs that the well-fixed in social work would have liked to ignore."[62]

These new activities led to a serious breach with her superior, Kimball. Their hitherto satisfactory division of labor in the school was shaken: "Now he began to say my influence brought to the school a type of student he did not want ('New York Jews,' he said brutally) when he preferred sleek daughters of the old families, 'the race horse type' whom he considered to be in the Smith College tradition."[63]

Kimball was terrified of group action and was very opposed to Reynolds's association with undignified social workers who went so far as to side with their clients in supporting trade unions. For her part, Reynolds had recognized his genteel anti-Semitism earlier, but now could no longer ignore it.

By now a forceful leader in the field, Reynolds felt further strengthened by her own recent successful psychoanalysis. She told Kimball he would have to accept her professional judgments or ask for her resignation. He complied, but it was clear that their relationship was heading for a break.

In part the rift between them was widened by what many contemporary students of social work consider to be Reynolds's greatest contribution, the development of a special program known as Plan D.[64] This was an attempt to create a program at the Smith College School for Social Work to train social work teachers and supervisors. Reynolds was concerned that the teaching skills she and others had developed would not be passed on to future generations. She also wanted an opportunity to synthesize two diverging fields—group work and psychiatric casework. She opted for resigning as associate director in order to organize the special Plan D training program. Kimball gave his grudging acquiescence but felt very threatened by any association or cooperation between group workers and case workers. Reynolds believed that he "wanted to cultivate the isolation of psychiatric treatment of individuals." [65]

An even greater crisis ensued when she supported a student revolt against a faculty member who had praised Hitler in his classes. When she refused to allow Plan D students to take this professor's course, it was clear she had pushed Kimball to the limit. He withdrew his support for Plan D and, essentially, forced her to resign from the Smith College School for Social Work, since there was no other opening at the school. The new associate director, Annette Garrett, who had been hired when Reynolds resigned to head up Plan D, told her that Kimball preferred a relationship with a woman associate director that allowed him to give and receive much more support than Reynolds had been willing to offer. Garrett went on to advise Reynolds that she should have been less independent in developing Plan D. The politic thing would have been to ask for his advice and to cultivate him much more. [66]

Reynolds's fight with Kimball can be seen in a variety

of ways. In part, as Garrett suggested, Reynolds had emerged as too independent and forceful for the conservative male figure who headed the school. Equally important were the growing ideological differences between them. He fully accepted the efficacy of the psychiatric casework approach, which never threatened the status quo. She became increasingly committed to integrating Marxist and Freudian thought and to developing a profession that brought together social and structural issues as well as personality development. Her departure from Smith in 1938 came at the height of her career, but it marked the beginning of her defeat. "I became a national figure in social work, not because of technical proficiency but for a philosophy that made one whole of professional practice and fine living, and inspired and uplifted many young workers."[67] She goes on to recall how short this effective period was: "From these years on I fought a losing fight against reactionary forces seeking to control social work, to drive it back to its island and corrupt its growing public services. I lost the security of a recognized position in social work and became a symbol of 'red' influence to be feared by those in authority in the profession. . . . The process was gradual beginning when I left Smith in 1938."[68]

## FINDING A PLACE IN THE
## PROFESSIONAL HIERARCHY

The school's decision to focus on the training of psychiatric social workers was initially a creative response to new possibilities for women's career development. The field of psychiatry was flowering, and many believed the new work in understanding the human psyche had radical possibilities for changing society's approach to social problems. Gaining support from the medical profession was crucial, since much of the early work was done in hospitals and asylums under the supervision of physicians.[69] By the time the relationship between social work and medicine had been worked out, the radical vision had been replaced by the increasing acceptance and Americanization of Freudian ideas and the understanding that social work would function largely as an accessible and subordinate rung in the medical hierarchy or be consigned to the lower status of administering public relief.

This resolution of the place of psychiatric social work in the medical hierarchy plagued the social work leaders from the earliest days. Even E. E. Southard, a strong advocate who had envisioned social workers socializing doctors, was worried about the status question. It was in the context of this struggle for control of the mental health market and the physicians' intention to control the area of mental health that Southard observed: "There is room in the world for the nurse, for the occupation workers, and for that main stay of reform, the competent secretarial aid. There is room for the woman technician in bacteriology and other sciences, and no one doubts that there is room for the social worker. It seems to me that we can say already on the basis of the didactic part of our Smith College–Boston State Hospital course that there is room for the psychiatric social worker too."[70]

In case this relegation to the company of secretaries and technicians was not enough to set fears at rest concerning the claims of the psychiatric social worker, Southard then shifted tactics. He reminded his readers that the "psychopath" was acknowledged as the central figure in "family problems." And, by way of giving the psychiatric social worker's aspirations final legitimacy, he pointed out that the "best of all is that these women [the social workers] have not only preserved their interest in the family" by training to treat the psychopath, "but have developed a wish to meet the psychopath and as it were 'grasp the nettle.'"[71] The chief male supporter of psychiatric social work for women ended by justifying that endeavor as an appropriate focus for female concern because women would, after all, really be engaged in solving family problems.

Unfortunately, such a justification played into society's assumptions and values concerning women's appropriate place. By emphasizing the identification with home and family, Southard tended to make the service, or altruistic, component of female professional endeavor a paramount concern and their main source of ideological legitimacy. This followed a long tradition of appealing to the ideology of service to justify women's work.

This tradition of service turned out to be both an asset and an obstacle to social workers' claim to be fully professional. It was an asset because it appropriated the historical pattern of female charitable service to the poor and the powerless, and in that way enjoyed the prestige that the settlement houses and friendly visitor movements had established by the end of the nineteenth century. These activities had paved the way for female entrance into the public sphere and had glorified women's charitable (unpaid) activities. But the commitment to service was also an obstacle because it was bound up with notions quite different from those most prized by the new professional culture. Service, especially when associated with charity, had the suspect quality of being freely given in a society increasingly propelled by profit motives; service placed high priority on nobility of feeling and concern for others in a society that insisted on associating affect with the unscientific and nonrational; service emphasized the need to nurture the unfortunate in a society, many of whose newly rich lacked even the paternalistic impulses of noblesse oblige. Altruistic motives were still praised by the professional culture but hardly prized by them.

In declaring that women's entry into social work was only the female role taken out of the family and put into the public sphere—that is, the galvanizing of nurturant, supportive behavior in the service of virtuous causes—women professionals drew the boundaries of their endeavors around areas that men were not apt to find attractive.[72] To that extent they defused male anxieties. But the combination of focusing on the least powerful elements of the society—the indigent, the sick, and the delinquent—and the emphasis on service as natural women's work set the groundwork for social work's subordination. The appointment to schools and agencies of male administrators who would support this limited subordinate role reinforced the likelihood that social work's professional authority would be circumscribed.

Many social workers, like Mary Jarrett and her students, continued to hold a deep and abiding faith that personal attention and professional concern would in fact improve their clients' intolerable circumstances. They retained the humanitarian component derived from an earlier tradition of the friendly visitor, even as they turned to psychiatry to distinguish their expertise from that of the volunteers. Despite their sincere dedication, many of these middle-class women continued to share a strong class bias and an increasingly powerful professional ideology that led them to define their clients as dependents. This ideology also prevented them from recognizing that these same clients could be potential allies in challenging their common exclusion from positions of power.

When Bertha Reynolds and some of her colleagues challenged these definitions during the Great Depression, they found themselves pushed to the margins or driven from the field. Psychiatric social workers were welcome in hospitals and social agencies only if they did not threaten the status quo. This meant that most agencies and schools would be run by men. It also meant that psychiatric social work would remain subordinate to medicine, in general, and to psychiatry in particular. Nor would psychiatric social work develop a critical stance on political issues of poverty or other social problems. Continued funding of these programs depended on maintaining a medical view of social illnesses.

## PRACTICING PROFESSIONALS

The establishment of the Smith College School for Social Work as a regular graduate program was intended not only to produce and train appropriate candidates, but also to serve as an institutional focus that monitored membership into the profession and exerted control over practitioners. In this battle social work was never completely victorious. Although the Smith School ultimately required a bachelor's degree as a prerequisite for its graduate training, it was not equally successful in eliminating workers who had no professional training from social work agencies. Participation by those who lacked proper credentials weakened the social workers' wider social authority and diminished their prestige.[73]

In the 1920s, when a full-scale graduate school at Smith College had been launched, it was still too early to anticipate some of these future problems. At that time the future looked promising. A number of graduates were working in the field, the fundamental character of the profession had been outlined, and many of the tensions could still be ignored in the hope that scientifically trained professionals could overcome most of the obstacles.[74]

The Smith School supporters adopted Mary Jarrett's belief that the casework method and individual therapy would provide their graduates with attributes and benefits comparable to their male counterparts. Yet psychiatric social work never gained control of a powerful institutional locus, as doctors had done in staking out the hospitals or researchers had done in claiming the universities. Nor did they win legal backing that would require their participation as experts in certain critical functions. They had no activity parallel to the admitting and discharging functions in hospitals, which could only be done by M.D.s, or to the granting of degrees, which was the prerogative of faculties. Instead, as social work focused increasingly on family welfare and relief work, it dealt with clienteles who were the least prestigious in the society.

As women, the social workers' power in the society at large was less than that of other professionals, and their power relationship with their clienteles reflected this subordination. In the hospital setting only physicians headed the hierarchically organized programs under which other professionals—including social workers—were subsumed. Even as the demand for therapists grew and the psychoanalytic content in the curriculum became more sophisticated, psychiatric social workers most often treated the clinic and welfare patients and psychiatrists treated the more affluent who could afford their services. Social workers operated through increasingly bureaucratic structures financed by public funding or by major philanthropists; the most prestigious psychiatrists practiced in private settings and received patient fees.[75]

Furthermore, even the most powerful women, such as Jarrett and Reynolds, found real limits to their ability to shape and define the graduate program they had helped to found. If they wanted to challenge the exclusive focus on psychological needs, as Reynolds did, they often found themselves at odds with the established leadership, who believed the greatest opportunities would come from working with other, more powerful mental health professionals and who were wary of defying business leaders responsible for funding many of the social welfare agencies. Further, because social workers did not work as independent professionals but in bureaucratic organizations, they often reported to superiors who had no training in social work but who were able to command authority by virtue of other credentials. When this occurred, female social workers were put in a subordinate relationship with male administrators, further eroding their claims to autonomy and exclusive expertise.[76]

In exploring the roots of the social workers' inability to achieve equal treatment with men, it is important not to overlook the founders' genuine achievements and contribution. Dedicated women such as Mary Jarrett elevated psychiatric social work into a paid occupation that was accessible to educated women. In fact, social work became one of the very few professional options for generations of educated women. By developing this career, the founders expanded the list of possible professions that had previously been limited to teaching, nursing, and librarianship. The development of another viable and socially useful field dominated by women was no small feat.

In responding to their exclusion from traditional areas of professional endeavor, these women chose to focus their energy, intelligence, and creativity on the unfortunate and submerged groups. Meeting their needs held the least reward, and their problems were often the most unyielding. These were not fields of enterprise that were apt to attract upwardly mobile, self-consciously professional men who sought the stunning breakthroughs, the clear-cut and readily measured accomplishments, and the clienteles that brought wealth and prestige to those who worked with them.

## CREATION OF PSYCHIATRIC SOCIAL WORK

This group of social work innovators were more far-sighted than some women who were attempting to make room for themselves in different professions. The social work leadership understood, as many others did not, that the creation of a graduate school was critical to the production of successive generations of professionals. What they were unable to confront, and perhaps could not under the circumstances, was the gathering strength of the forces outside the graduate school that were working against them—their vulnerability in a situation that required them to compete with other professionals who were obtaining tight control over the membership at the expense of service ideals and meritocratic standards. They were continually criticized for not having a clear theoretical foundation that distinguished their expertise from those in other fields. This led to considerable status anxiety on the part of social workers who were always searching for their true mission. What they failed to realize is that the more powerful professions first eliminated competition and then often determined their intellectual contributions as the field developed.

But the fierce requirements of eliminating competition and monopolizing control over certain crucial services was a style that had little or no social accretion or tradition among women. Social workers pinned their hopes on the efficacy of personal dedication, on an ideology of service and merit, as well as on a "scientifically" based case methodology, and often ignored or misjudged their need for wider reservoirs of power. Social workers learned that their best chance of thriving was not to threaten others who had more power than they

did. They found that when some of their members, like
Bertha Reynolds, moved to engage in political activity
that broadened the scope of professional responsibility,
they were often shunned by the profession and left without a crucial institutional base. Recognizing the dangers
inherent in challenging the power structure, they did
what they thought was possible at the time. They succeeded in establishing professional graduate training for
women by women. They believed, with good reason,
that this was an active and creative solution to prejudice
against educated women. It was a socially conscious
rather than a self-aggrandizing response that required
initiative and ability. They may have been willing to accept the subordination of psychiatric social workers to
physicians or bureaucratic administrators, but they never
accepted the notion of women as passive victims of
prejudice.

# A VIEW FROM
# THE MARGINS

These nine were remarkable women. They managed to forge successful careers in different institutional settings and, for the most part, acquired substantial reputations in their fields. They came of age at the height of the Progressive period, when many were dazzled by the expansion of new opportunities, the culture of social reform, and the growing enthusiasm for technical expertise. Increased availability of college education for women, the development of new graduate schools, the formation of new associations, and the creation of new positions gave them a sense of possibility and entitlement and provided a focus for their ambition and growing expertise.

The prejudice and discrimination they faced as women must have seemed inevitable but not paralyzing. They grew up in the last decades of the nineteenth century, after all, when women were bombarded with signals that told them to define their own roles in a sphere separate from men. In the new society, industrialized and urbanized, women were emerging as consumers, as managers in the home, and as volunteers who kept church and charitable organizations functioning. Even where they forged new options, such as the women's colleges, the settlement houses, the women's clubs, or the suffrage organizations, they tended to do so largely in the company of other women.

These nine women, along with many of their classmates and colleagues, knew, without any special instruction, that their experience would be radically different from their brothers, despite their shared social class and religious background. What marked them as special, and so suitable for their pioneering roles, was a belief that they could forge a synthesis between the Progressive sense of burgeoning opportunities and the separate, more constricted world of female endeavor. It was to be education and scientific expertise that would allow them to play new roles and exercise their social, moral, and intellectual concerns in new arenas.

None of these women sat down and chose to be a superperformer or an innovator, as one would choose to be a physician or social worker. Yet it quickly became clear to them that entrance into the elite world of professionalism would require special strategies for women. Limited admissions, the known prejudice against women, the lack of role models all signaled to the Reeds and the Sabins that extraordinary performance was crucial to gain acceptance into professional arenas and to legitimize their commitment to a career.

For other women the gender stratification of professional life often created opportunities in certain female-dominated fields, such as botany or social work, that were viable and attractive. Women who moved in these directions never saw themselves accepting a subordinate role. Often the new positions offered creative options—the possibility for women to exert leadership in areas that badly needed the concern of able professionals, whether that help was offered to returning veterans or to victims of lead poisoning.

Only in retrospect do we see how narrow the range of options really was. Most women could not expect a full and successful career even if they performed competently in the training and apprentice periods. Even the most talented and ambitious women were not considered for leadership positions and normally had little leverage in the development of professional structures or graduate education.

The strategies of superperformance, separatism, innovation, and subordination were so pervasive and so influential for future generations of professionals that it is worth a further look at them. In the case studies we examined superperformance in medicine, separatism in the women's colleges, innovation in science and public health, and subordination in social work. But no strategy was limited to one profession. Examples of superperformance abounded in all fields. Some women in science chose subordination; others chose it in academic settings where they served as lecturers and research associates all their lives. Most women found that one strategy was not sufficient in managing their careers over the entire life cycle. They might rely on superperformance in graduate school and then go on to innovation in the work setting. Reconstructing a history of the times we can see that women were involved in every creative strategy that could serve their larger purpose of building meaningful careers.

## SUPERPERFORMANCE

Superperformance was an obvious approach: women sought professional status through extraordinary efforts and performance. They overcame barriers by dint of hard work, outstanding ability, and their willingness to sacrifice traditional relationships for their careers. Very few of the women who reached the highest places married; many were willing to forego the conventional boundaries of private life. Since they had no children and tended to be geographically removed from their families of origin, relations with colleagues served as their principal social and familial outlet.[1]

In the professional woman's determination to be recognized as the equal of her male counterpart, the superperformer of the early twentieth century was indefatigable. No task was too arduous, dangerous, time-consuming, or repugnant. Like Josephine Baker charging up the stairs of a fetid slum apartment and physically assaulting the drunken husband who obstructed her way to her laboring patient,[2] or Alice Hamilton interviewing in unventilated factories with no protection from free-floating lead dust the palsied and brain-damaged victims of lead poisoning, these professionals persisted in completing difficult and risky assignments.[3]

For the small minority who married, the situation was much more complex. Superperformance extended to their roles as mothers and wives even more than to that of professional. These women went to great lengths to avoid any intimation that they were somehow shirking their duty as mothers and wives. When their husbands' careers required it, they arranged for any necessary moves, smoothed over any irregularities in the schedule, entertained new associates, and ameliorated any pressures that were felt in the household. As a result these superperformers often found their own career am-

bitions repositioned at the end of a long line of other demands. Sometimes they had to retreat from their highest
goals, accept a more subordinate role, or move into a
new kind of work that dovetailed more easily with their
domestic obligations.

## SUBORDINATION

In addition to married women, many other able women
who attempted to work in fields that absolutely prohibited them or who did not have the privilege of the
best education opted to work as assistants or in other
subordinate positions. In essence, subordination meant
accepting positions of lesser rank in male-dominated
fields. This was the case with female astronomers who
were hired to record data and do all the tedious measure-
ments and calculations on the understanding that they
could never be promoted to faculty rank.[4]

Many women found such positions attractive because
they provided professional employment, which was often
scarce. At the same time, a subordinate response obvi-
ated the need to compete with men or to justify such
competition. While male supervisors welcomed women
as research assistants and incorporated many good ideas
that subordinates contributed, they were resistant to
giving women public credit or offering them equal rewards. Director of the Harvard College Observatory,
Edward Pickering, justified to the Harvard overseers his
employment of a score of female assistants by pointing
out that "Many of the assistants are skillful only in their
own particular work, but are nevertheless capable of

doing as much good routine work as astronomers who would receive much larger salaries. Three or four times as many assistants can thus be employed, and the work done correspondingly increased for a given expenditure."[5]

Even some of the most determined superperformers justified the creation and elaboration of these subordinate positions. Women such as Mary Woolley, president of Mount Holyoke, were hard pressed to find adequate employment for their graduates and used every means possible to encourage the creation of new opportunities; Woolley was even willing to have them serve as permanent assistants and technicians if nothing else were available.[6] For the same reason Maria Mitchell, the nationally famous astronomer at Vassar College, encouraged her students to pursue the female-designated jobs in astronomy.[7] These groundbreakers recognized that there were limits to the number of superperformers they could graduate. This was equally true for men's institutions, but the consequences were very different for men and women. A competent man, helped along by family support and institutional structures, was entitled to a full-fledged professional career. Everyone expected the average male physician to build a practice and acquire appropriate staff affiliations with hospitals. The qualified Ph.D. anticipated that his work, if decent, would be rewarded by promotion up the faculty ranks. Women, by contrast, were always under pressure to demonstrate their extraordinary qualities and excellence in order to justify their competition with men for full participation and rewards. If they had merely ordinary ability, convention required that they serve as assistants or, better still, stay at home.

In their eagerness to create places for the largest possible number of competent educated women, female leaders sometimes formulated an ideology that justified certain activities as peculiarly feminine specialties, presumed to respond to women's special, "natural" abilities. This strategy was advocated by Williamina Fleming, curator of astronomical photographs and supervisor of the research assistants at Harvard. "While we cannot maintain that in everything woman is man's equal," she wrote in 1893, "yet in many things her patience, perseverance, and method make her his superior."[8]

Still a different pattern of subordination developed in female-dominated professions. In fields such as nursing or psychiatric social work, the entire occupation was in fact dominated by an allied but more powerful male profession, which supplied supervision and circumscribed female autonomy. Psychiatric social workers, no matter how experienced or competent, always deferred to the authority of the psychiatrist. His superiority was reinforced by his capacity to write prescriptions and hospitalize patients. Nurses, who had the most intense and prolonged interactions with hospital patients, still had to rely on the supervising doctor to initiate specific procedures in the management of the case.

The struggle for control was particularly evident in public health nursing and the physician's response to it. A recent study of the history of nursing documents the fact that "physicians opposed public health work in defense of their own prerogatives." The author goes on to point out that the "lay movement threatened doctors' claims to the exclusive right to define the content and organization of medical care, to control related services, and to work without constraints from outsiders." In 1924 one doctor made this quite explicit when he publicly complained about "the aggressiveness of the public health nurse."[9]

Unlike the astronomers or other research scientists, there were no restraints on individual promotions within the ranks of the subordinate career; but even if a capable woman could be promoted to head nurse, she would still be subordinate in the health profession and operate from a highly circumscribed autonomy.

Working in a subordinate profession was not all bad. Because subordinate jobs were clustered in particular areas designated as appropriate for women, the positions were not defined by those in power as incompatible with marriage. A nurse or teacher would not normally be accused of wasting her education if she decided to marry, but a doctor would be. Equally attractive was the potential for the companionship of co-workers. Unlike the superperformer, who was often the token woman in an all-male setting and excluded from extraprofessional activities designed for men, women in subordinate professions could count on the sociability and support of other women. This more comfortable social situation, combined with the sense that they were helping the poor and the needy, may have played an important role in reinforcing an individual's reluctance to challenge the barriers. Subordination reaffirmed the idea that work was essentially sex segregated. Under these conditions women could render excellent service. Unfortunately, it did not entitle them to equality with men.

## INNOVATION

The third strategy—innovation—was used by women who were drawn deliberately or by chance to new fields of interest. Often, but not necessarily, these areas were paid poorly, served lower-class clients, and did not attract many men. As innovators began to formulate these new positions, their career patterns were not clear. Psychiatric social work, for example, began as a creative innovation on the part of women such as Mary Jarrett. When Jarrett began her training institute at Smith College in 1918, she was not sure what career possibilities would exist after the war. Inventing as she went along, she struggled to broaden the opportunities for future social workers.

Innovators tended to remove themselves from direct competition with male professionals in two ways. One way, in the missionary tradition, involved physical relocation to remote and often exotic places. Thus, we saw Anne Walter Fearn set up a hospital in China that offered a wide range of medical services to local populations. Similarly, the settlement houses, a preprofessional alternative largely populated by female college graduates, required women to relocate to urban slums that were almost as foreign to the life-style of these middle-class women as the city of Shanghai was to someone such as Fearn.[10]

Women also avoided competition with men by moving into areas ignored by the established professions. When Alice Hamilton left her position as a bacteriologist in a laboratory to investigate conditions in factories that used poisonous minerals and chemicals, there had never been so much as a conference or a single issue of a scientific journal devoted to industrial medicine.[11] There was no established career trajectory for this occupation, no sense of the next rung on the career ladder, and perhaps no ladder at all. If Hamilton's work involved personal jeopardy as she investigated hazardous work sites, it also involved career risks. At first she had to be willing to offer her expertise for no pay. It was left to her to resolve how to proceed when her first Illinois survey was completed. When she began she did not know she would be asked to follow that statewide investigation with a national survey, and even this research, commissioned by the federal government, provided no salary until it was completed.[12]

Because many professional women, like Hamilton, were middle class and single, they had fewer personal responsibilities. And if married, these women were ordinarily earning the second salary in the family. Thus professional women had greater financial flexibility, which perhaps spurred them to enter into high-risk ventures in new fields without being too concerned about the income they would earn. On the other hand, the fact that money was not their primary concern often made them overly eligible for ill-paid jobs that tended to be clustered on the margins of professional life. Their willingness to accept less money widened the gap between them and their male colleagues, who felt preoccupied with their financial responsibilities as breadwinners. Women's tendency to deny that money was a principal motivation in their professional lives exacerbated the men's resentment. Men saw them as less serious persons who were dabbling in careers without any understanding of the pressures to succeed financially.

Despite the disparaging attitudes of some contemporaries, many women who served the needy populations made significant contributions. The professionals who worked with the Children's Bureau and public health agencies to reduce infant and maternal mortality may have been poorly paid and viewed with disdain, yet their long-run impact on health standards was considerable. Women such as Dorothy Reed or Josephine Baker served as forerunners in fields that blossomed a generation later.[13]

## SEPARATISM

The separatists shared many of the goals and attributes of the other groups; still they form a distinct category because they emphasized the special possibilities of female-controlled institutions. Given the choice between a lesser position in a larger, male-dominated organization or a paramount position in a smaller female enclave, the separatists saw the advantages of the latter. In separate institutions women would control decision making.

Separatism took the idea of separate spheres and transformed it to the benefit of women. While the separatists understood that for most women there was a rigid division between public and private activity, this particular formulation of separatism permitted some women to define and create a special and exclusively female public sphere. Clearly, this reversed conventional ideas about which gender should predominate in the public sphere.

Separatist scholars did not remain in the home nor even try to excel in both spheres. For them public, professional life was the priority, and they constructed their domestic lives as an accompaniment to the demands of their careers.

Separatists worked primarily in single-sex institutions, but this did not lessen their desire to maintain the full rigor of professional commitment as the leading men in the field were defining it. They wanted their students to be as well trained as any coming out of major universities; they wanted their books to be reviewed in the most important journals and their research to be on the cutting edge of their respective fields. It is only by understanding this determination that we can fully appreciate Mary Woolley's decision, as early as 1901, to assemble a faculty of women Ph.D.s at Mount Holyoke in an era when few college faculties anywhere could meet such elevated standards.

The northeastern women's colleges have been the subject of any number of studies that have emphasized their special role as producers of talented women and their changing definitions of how this should be done.[14] What is more germane to our purpose is their significant role as the continuous employers of professional women. For some fields, such as physics or math, the women's colleges represented virtually the only possible employer of female professionals. Several of the colleges' important leaders, Mary Woolley and M. Carey Thomas among others, were fully aware of the need to foster opportunities for the ongoing professional development of their faculties. The most ambitious among the women presidents ferreted out every possibility. They cajoled, bargained, and pleaded to obtain adequate financial resources to fund postgraduate work, sabbaticals, and professional meetings and to build a general endowment that would secure the future of their institutions. Even in the less overtly feminist colleges for women, where the president was a man and the faculty made up of both men and women, there were greater opportunities for female advancement than any coeducational institution would offer.[15]

The women's colleges provided opportunities for leadership development and accelerated the professional activities of female scholars; still, building a homogeneous enclave at institutions such as Mount Holyoke, Bryn Mawr, and Wellesley involved costly trade-offs. For some women the single-sex community that evolved in these circumstances seemed enormously attractive and more satisfying than they thought marriage could ever be. But for others the choice of a professional career undoubtedly involved considerable sacrifice in giving up marriage and especially the opportunity to have children. What the separatists failed to address was the durability of marriage and motherhood as compelling traditions that were reinforced by all the major structures in society. Although the majority of women students always saw college as an interlude before marriage, during the first three decades of the twentieth century substantial numbers of young women were socialized to accept the virtues of professionalism and scholarship over marriage.

But the need of the colleges to operate in the larger

world undermined their long-term capacity to resist these pressures. Even Mary Woolley, a woman who had no personal doubts about rejecting marriage, had to moderate her goals for future graduates by assuring the public that Mount Holyoke graduates would possess special female qualities and service ideals. No matter how different or separate her campus community seemed to be, as college president she constantly had to persuade a variety of groups, ranging from parents to directors of funding agencies to the undergraduates themselves, that her college was preparing graduates of whom they would approve.[16]

Ultimately the disjuncture between professional and traditional subcultures in the college could not be contained, and the separatist life-style that Woolley and her followers represented came under hostile scrutiny and divisive attack. It was in this context that the trustees replaced Woolley—that ambitious leader who spearheaded the creation of a first-rank college—with a man whom many perceived to be conventional and bland. It was a struggle that produced embittered feelings among faculty, students, and alumnae alike.[17] Nonetheless, the efforts of those such as Woolley and Thomas helped establish a tradition of scholarly excellence and professional possibilities for women.

## THE IMPACT OF THE FOUR STRATEGIES

Most of the women whose lives we have examined overcame the chief obstacles facing them and managed to achieve illustrious careers. The success of these individual women should not obscure the negative consequences that resulted from women's forced reliance on these limited strategies. Often their victories were accompanied by their own recognition that such success was exceptional and that they could rarely pave the way for the larger number of women behind them. Furthermore, women struggling for acceptance in the male-dominated environment that professional life represented did not challenge the ideology of professional life, even when they experienced serious injustices.

In confronting the prejudice against them—lower salaries, discrimination in appointments and promotions, systematic assumption of power and status by men—women professionals recognized the persistence of long-term historical patterns. They tried to respond to these inequities; sometimes they organized separate institutions or lobbied for more equal treatment. But this was quite distinct from challenging the premises of professsonalism itself, from questioning hierarchical structures or the growing public sentiment that allowed professionals to serve as social arbiters and to speak on a wide variety of public issues, not just as citizens but as presumed experts.

Like most aspiring professionals, women believed that the occupations they had chosen were characterized by two predominant characteristics: meritocracy and objectivity. Meritocacy assumed equality of opportunity based on ability. All professionals would have to master an abstract body of knowledge and hold to an ideal of service. Objectivity required that self-interest be subordinated to the societal good. Certainly all persons would be eligible for the same diagnosis in the doctor's office and the same treatment in the courts or classroom. These basic features would in the long run protect both professionals and clients from the worst abuses.

With historical hindsight we can see that this process of professionalization entailed a restructuring of the educational process to incorporate new intellectual formulations, and it put the scientific method at the center of expertise.[18] Equally important was the need to restrict the supply of candidates and eliminate competitors. At the same time, many leading professionals linked themselves with capitalists and philanthropists. These people had the power to underwrite the professionals' drive to develop institutions where they could define and distribute professional services.

This process turned out to be highly prejudicial to women, minorities, and immigrants, who were seen as intruders and interlopers, not fit for this new work. No conspiracy is implied; no conspiracy was needed. Just as women did not have prescience about the consequences of the strategies they formulated, but took whatever opportunities the situation provided, so professional leaders who were men looked to their natural networks and contacts to build hospitals, graduate schools, laboratories, and other professional institutions. It is no surprise that they also benefited from the predominant beliefs in the larger society about the superiority of white, native-born men as leaders in these endeavors.

The prejudices of male leaders were not focused solely on women. In fact, in many fields leaders believed the larger threat was posed by immigrants and Jews. To cite just one example of how these prejudices operated to limit those of unacceptable ethnicity, gender, or race, we might look at a study of the modernization of the legal profession. In the development of the American Bar Association we can see how exclusivity and discrimination were at the very core of the professionalizing process for lawyers.

In his study of the legal profession Gerald Auerbach shows that the emergence of the modern legal profession was similar in its development to other occupations that we examined. The establishment of the corporate firm lawyer as the most prestigious practitioner, the American Bar Association's successful push to become the law profession's protective guild, and the triumph of the new university professors who succeeded in introducing the case method as the foundation of scientific legal education together formed the core of the modern legal profession.[19]

There were several threats to the elite leadership of the corporate lawyers and the professors of the prestigious, university-based law schools. These men were unnerved by the prospect of being inundated by Eastern European immigrants, and especially by Jews. For example, Auerbach quoted one prominent Pennsylvania attorney who acknowledged that while Jews might be "intellectually gifted and persevering," these qualities did not make Jews acceptable because they did not have the "incalculable advantage of having been brought up in American family life" and could "hardly be taught the ethics of the profession as adequately as we desire."[20] This argument echoes statements about women being too emotional and too lacking in objectivity to function effectively in professional life, irrespective of the quality of their performance in classes and examinations.

The legal reformers were unsuccessful in their bid to imitate the medical reformers by closing down the night and proprietary schools attended by immigrants. Instead, they prolonged the training period and increased the cost, hoping thus to limit law school to those who could afford the greater financial outlay. In addition, a number of leaders advocated stratifying the profession so that the undesirables who penetrated the bar were restricted to probate work, criminal law, and trial practice and kept out of the more lucrative and prestigious corporate law, judgeships, and access to important political positions.[21]

The major law schools did not keep Jews out permanently, although for a long time the schools were successful in limiting their penetration into the most elite firms. Law schools were even more effective in prohibiting the entrance of women. By 1963 women accounted for only 2.7 percent of the profession. In the early 1980s, after a major push begun in the previous decade, women constituted about a third of the students.[22] The treatment of blacks followed the same pattern, but was even more extreme. For a period of two decades or more, some states failed all black candidates for the bar.[23]

Auerbach's case study of the legal profession makes it clear that discrimination was diffuse and widespread. The women we have studied were caught in a much larger pattern of prejudice and discrimination. What was special about their situation was that their middle-class status prevented them from identifying with these other excluded groups or from challenging the concept of merit and achievement as the cornerstone to professional achievement.

## THE IDEOLOGY OF MERIT AND DISINTERESTED SERVICE

It should be no surprise that the women we have studied were committed to an ideology of merit. It was entirely in keeping with their training to accept and incorporate the new professional ideology that stressed two basic premises above all—merit and disinterested service. They were aware of the social and historical context of their own place in society. They knew that other traditional methods of recruitment into desired positions relied even more on patronage and power relationships from which they had normally been excluded. White women of the middle class were well positioned to compete for relatively scarce places if it meant succeeding in tests or meeting other universal standards of performance.

Their faith in merit was further reinforced by the success of some of the most visible women. Nellie Neilson and Bertha Putnam, American and female, reached the apex of the virtually all-male world of English medieval institutional history. The medical research of a Florence Sabin earned her the respect of the scientific community nationally. Alice Hamilton's successes in industrial medicine caused the otherwise obdurate brotherhood of the Harvard Medical School to appoint her to the faculty.

The list could be elaborated with hundreds of other illustrations: Maria Mitchell in astronomy to Cornelia Clapp in botany, Mary van Kleeck in public policy, and Ruth Benedict in anthropology.[24]

These successes continued to strengthen female professionals' belief that if they were only good enough, ultimately they would have to be given professional recognition; their attachment to this idea persisted even when they were bypassed for deserved appointments and promotions or subjected to endless petty tyrannies.

What was justifiably difficult for them to understand in this situation was the inevitable tension between the professional culture's commitment to merit and its need to control a monopoly of services in any given field. When the male leadership made an aggressive bid to control the clients as well as the members of a profession, it did not stop to weigh the advantages of a more pluralistic occupational structure, one that might be capable of producing better service or of embracing the best practitioners from all groups. The decision to maintain merit, but subordinate it in favor of professional control, meant that apprentice or night school lawyers might possibly be fit for ambulance chasing and family court, but were definitely barred from Wall Street; midwives had to give way to obstetricians, even if some rural areas were short of doctors.[25] One of the major scholars of the medical profession has aptly summarized the consequences of these practices.

In the wake of the Flexner report medicine became a staunchly middle-class occupation, centered on the towns and cities. If in the process the poor boy were denied access to medicine as a profession, if the standards were made so rigid that the gifted were sometimes excluded, if in the long run it might have been advantageous to the health care of the American people to continue to train a vast spectrum of doctors ranging from medical scientists to rural practitioners, these were small considerations at the time. Success was to be measured in the rising status of the doctor, in the excellence of the leading schools, and in the unification through the A.M.A. of the professional institutions of medicine.[26]

What was most remarkable was how successfully the ideologists of the profession continued to insist that standards—and by extension merit—had the highest priority in admissions and distribution of the necessary perquisites of professional success: hospital admitting and discharging privileges, journal access, and privileged communications. Because monopoly practices were based on gender and race, they worked against women in a way that the victims could neither fully comprehend nor overcome.

Professional ideals also required that true professionals should serve the greater social good, which meant that one's expertise should be offered to those in need, irrespective of their ability to pay. For women, who already had a long tradition of unpaid service for charitable purposes, this expectation was particularly attractive. The capacity to assuage the misery of the needy and to nurture the downtrodden in an increasingly impersonal society often provided the necessary legitimacy for women to move from the home into the marketplace.

In their willingness, and indeed optimistic eagerness, to incorporate new clients as the beneficiaries of professional service, women failed to perceive the connection between the lower status of those they served, often the poor and the powerless, and the meager rewards that they as professionals would receive. Poor clients could not afford to pay. If male psychiatrists and corporate lawyers carved out their territory to serve those who could afford to pay well, women professionals such as social workers, public health officials, or public interest lawyers were often left to service the rest and to scramble for uncertain payment. Even when women understood that they were paying a high professional price for their strict adherence to an ideology of disinterested service, the appeal of humanitarian goals often prevailed.

Many male and female professionals were divided on their degree of commitment to service ideology. Seldom was this more graphically presented than in the instance of the testimony given before the Sheppard congressional committee hearing in the early 1920s, reported by Josephine Baker in her autobiography. She described the testimony of the young doctor from the New England Medical Society, concerned that the emphasis of the Children's Bureau on public health would end the inducement for young men to study medicine because the number of potentially sick patients would decrease. We saw a similar phenomenon when Dorothy Reed was advised by her Wisconsin fellow physicians to think of medicine as a business and not as a service.[27]

These unvarnished remarks reveal the tension between service goals and the drive for total professional control that focused on more affluent clients. Joyce Antler, in her study of professional women, points out that the correlation between gender and altruism versus power was never exact. Obviously, some prominent men tried to introduce humane service considerations into increasingly exclusive professionalized fields, not only in medicine, but also in social work and the social sciences. Similarly, Regina Morantz has documented the controversy among female professional leaders over the appropriateness of a service versus a scientific orientation.[28]

Despite individual variation among men and women, the overwhelming thrust of male professional life subordinated service considerations and rewarded those who pursued "careerist" goals and the "main chance." When these two objectives became incompatible, women, who constituted the more marginal group, often chose merit and service, while the male-dominated professional organizations ordinarily opted first for the rewards of professional control.

## FOR WANT OF PROGENY

Although the strategies of superperformance, subordination, creative response, and separatism and the commitment to merit and service often worked well for the individual women achievers, seldom were they able to secure their hard won places for future generations. Lacking access to the structures that could facilitate their careers, each generation of women had to start anew. Female neophytes had to be prepared de novo to expend the energy and offer personal sacrifices as if a previous generation of pioneers had not already proven that women could be excellent contributors to the profession. By contrast their male counterparts provided growing opportunities and institutionalized patronage practices for younger men through mentor relationships and informal informational networks as well as through the formal powers of selection they held on licensing boards, in senior partnerships, and in high administrative posts.

Essentially women failed to achieve the kind of leverage that would have allowed them to assist their future progeny for two reasons. First, not enough women were well placed in powerful positions. The few women who did succeed were caught between the continued need to prove and reprove their own worthiness and the isolation of being token professionals. Because there were so few women professionals, it was impossible to have women represented on all the important decision-making bodies in sufficient numbers to affect policy favorable to future aspirants.[29] As tokens, even the most talented women such as Florence Sabin or Alice Hamilton remained vulnerable to the negative consequences of high visibility. They had to be sensitive to an everpresent scrutiny of their performance, personal style, and presentation of self.

This high degree of visibility and vulnerability had led aspiring women to look for ways to play down their gender. Dr. Mary Engle Pennington, for example, was a bacteriological chemist who did significant work on refrigeration of food for the Department of Agriculture. She was fortunate to have a male mentor, Dr. Harvey Wiley, who encouraged her career. He urged her to take the civil service examinations, but recognizing that her gender might present some difficulty, he suggested that she fill out her applications as M. E. Pennington, without calling attention to her first name. By the time they realized she was a woman, he argued, they would find there was no legal precedent for removing her from the position.[30] Pennington was fortunate to have someone to encourage her and guide her through the process. But not everyone did. Deciding what name to use and how to dress were constant nuisances; they required extra effort in unproductive areas that neither enhanced the quality of women's professional work nor offered the political opportunities to assist future generations.

Second, women were not ordinarily invited to participate in the decision-making committees. One reason contemporary proponents of affirmative action insist on representation of women and minorities on every committee is that they have come to understand that only physical presence can guarantee that applicants from minority groups will receive serious attention and not become subject to the derisive joke that undermines the outsider.

Even women who were very determined to help bring along the next generation were often foiled in their efforts. We might view the frequent occasions of petty, and seemingly irrational, humiliations as a system of signals intended to telegraph to the women that they were politically subordinate even if intellectually equal. What other construction should we put on Harvard's outrageous conditions when it employed the first female faculty member? Clearly, Alice Hamilton's presence or absence at the faculty club, the football games, and in the academic processions had little bearing on her effectiveness as teacher or scholar; but the university's insistence on these prohibitions served as a clear announcement to her and to others that women could not expect political power in the university and would be accepted only under extraordinary circumstances.[31]

Securing positions for the next generation was inhibited further by the standards of selection applied to women. Only women exceptionally able in their fields were ever recruited. Men, by contrast, were sometimes chosen as much for their administrative and leadership potential as for their expertise and were often schooled for future leadership positions. Dr. William Welch, for example, the first dean of the Johns Hopkins Medical School, is regarded as a legendary figure in the history of modern medicine. Although he was quite well trained for the period, his reputation was not built primarily on his contributions to medical research. Rather, he appears to have been selected on the basis of his class background and his potential for organizing and anticipating the directions in which modern medicine would develop.[32]

By contrast, if a woman displayed leadership potential or behavior that appeared too aggressive, she was often deemed unacceptable. Even in those instances where women, such as M. Carey Thomas or Mary Woolley, managed to have successful careers as administrators and thereby to create future opportunities for others, they did so by operating in all-female enclaves; more important, they never ceased to be suspect. In Woolley's case her opponents breathed a sigh of relief when she was replaced by a man, although he had had an unexceptional career at Yale, was considered by many to be an ineffectual administrator, and was committed to replacing women faculty members with young men.[33] The inability of female professionals to develop a pool of women with political and organizational skills further exacerbated the problem of producing progeny.

## THE PROBLEM OF EXPERTISE

Professionals have long claimed that scientific knowledge and scientific method together formed the bedrock on which professional activity and influence are based. Science offered the incontestable features of predictability, reliability, and validity. The rise of modern science and the decline of religion marked a major intellectual shift at the end of the nineteenth century. With this new *mentalité,* science was seen as the key to a series of modern possibilities—controlling the environment, harnessing new forms of energy, solving human problems, and accelerating social progress.

This unbridled infatuation with science permeated the politics of the society in ways that often had undemocratic consequences. For example, the eugenicists, while not the most extreme example of racists, nevertheless believed that humankind could be scientifically ranked according to racial characteristics. It was their claim to a scientific base for a program of "selective breeding" that enhanced their power to influence public policy and acquire substantial resources for their brand of research. The social engineers were certain that their scientific superiority entitled them to make economic and political choices that substituted technical expertise for a traditional belief in the judgment of ordinary people. In the workplace the enthusiasm for scientific management ultimately led to speedups on assembly lines and loss of worker autonomy.[34]

In the development of the professions this romance with all things scientific took a different form. Those who were able to claim scientific authority were in a highly advantageous position. They could monopolize the crucial mechanisms of professional life, especially control of the graduate schools and the training process, the professional codes and associations, research and dissemination of knowledge, and applications of future expertise.[35] Even where scientific expertise offered more promise than actual accomplishment, the claim to scientific knowledge was empowering.

The rising power of science was so broad, in fact, that in the scholarly and professional worlds it extended far beyond its usual associations with laboratory research. Even in humanistic fields such as social work and law there was a fascination with science.[36] Social work leaders and lawyers were convinced that the use of the case method would lead to the discovery of the scientific laws of human behavior. A scientifically based curriculum in social work and law was thought to give substantive rigor and discipline to fields that, in fact, had a scant scientific base.

Recent scholarship has ably examined the implications of the uncritical adoption of "scientific superiority" which provided the raison d'être for such ventures as phrenology, eugenics, Taylorism, and other forms of domination.[37] There has been less examination, however, of the impact of this value shift on women and other marginal or excluded groups in the professions. To understand more precisely how this faith in all things scientific operated against women in the professions, it is helpful to consider the way in which scientific beliefs functioned not only in the controlled environment of the laboratory, but also in the professional marketplace.

Many believed science would eliminate disease and other evils. The medical profession, for example, often promised that miracle cures would emerge from scientific research; but it was equally true, if less touted, that the much heralded miracle cure of one day could well be the iatrogenic disease of the next. The scientific truth of one day, which in many cases became the source of substantial social power, could well become the next day's anachronism, with devastating consequences for those who had ridden in on its crest.

There was an additional and unnerving possibility in the promotion of a particular group's scientific expertise. One of the hallmarks of such expertise was the clear recognition that these were vast areas of knowledge about which little or nothing was known. By the very act of staking out territories and boundaries for each discipline and for each applied profession, scientists acknowledged that there were significant boundaries to what any expert could comprehend. Even among the immensely sophisticated physicists of the 1980s, for example, knowledge about the origins of the universe and its geophysical future soon turns to speculation and controversy. In the early twentieth century the limits of scientific understanding were much greater.

Further, in many of the professions, expertise meant

applying scientific knowledge to particular problems. In such cases the professional often had to make decisions without having the ability to control all the variables. Practitioners were often required to make choices with very partial evidence. Lack of certainty easily produced insecurity among practitioners, who continually had to squelch their doubts about their abilities to solve the problems before them. In the face of cancer or polio or schizophrenia or persistent poverty or earthquakes, professionals who were unable to produce the needed solutions had to assure themselves that their expertise was at least relatively greater than that of other groups. In a study of the French hospital system, for example, Jamous and Peloille have shown how practitioners tended to resolve the tension resulting from uncertainty by mystifying the subject matter and emphasizing the creative or intuitive talent that took over at the point where technical expertise ceased.[38] By speaking in technical jargon and by using a patronizing tone, the professional signaled to the patient that something important was going on, but that the uninitiated would be unable to judge the quality of the performance.

The experts' nervous awareness of the fragility of science was heightened by the tendency of leading members of the field to leave the routine, more predictable work to their subordinates and to move their own practices into areas at the outer limits of knowledge, where intuition and chance play an even larger role. Professionals were never entirely free from the fear that a new finding, which they might not control, would publicly reveal that the "emperor had no clothes." This possibility often led to a closing of the ranks among professionals and encouraged a fear of outsiders who might conceivably threaten the basis of their expertise and, indeed, the entire fabric of their legitimacy. In this context we can better understand why so many professionals tempered their commitment to meritocracy in favor of recruiting homogeneous colleagues.

This process had profound consequences for women; women were highly visible and not easily absorbed into the homogeneous pool preferred by men who did not want new colleagues to question the rules of their game. Recruiting like-minded people of similar race, gender, and social background helped men ensure a reference group in which ideas could be telegraphed quickly and easily through a mutually understood style of presentation.

The experience of the young doctor Reed graphically illustrates a situation in which local professionals preferred homogeneous colleagues in order to veil some of the gaping holes in their expert services. Reed was among the best-trained physicians in the country when she married and moved from New York to Madison, Wisconsin. It was hard for her to tell whether the physicians there disliked her more for her gender or for her superior training and ability to question some of their daily practices. Her efforts at establishing some early health centers and well-baby clinics in Madison were not well received. In her memoirs she wrote that

In spite of the fact that I was not in practice and have not been paid one cent for medical services in my entire life—

this excludes, of course, salary for teaching and writing—
the medical profession of Madison has been unfriendly
to the work of the health centers from the very start. Of
course I was a woman and from the east, but public health
work was new to most physicians and seemed to the majority of the profession in Madison a distinct effort to undermine their means of livelihood.[39]

Public health, in effect, represented exactly the kind of
challenge to the physicians' authority that raised questions about their claim to the greatest professional expertise and their ability to control health care through
their private practices.

Sociologist Rosabeth Kanter has analyzed an analogous problem among contemporary executives in large
organizations. These high-ranking managers, far removed from any actual production in the contemporary
corporation, spend a great deal of time as facilitators,
communicating between various departments, supervising personnel, and managing tension. The higher they
climb on the organizational ladder, the more their work
becomes process oriented, so it becomes virtually impossible to evaluate their impact on productivity, sales,
or profits. Their skills depend on a particular presentation of self and can actually lack a substantive core. Kanter found that they often compensate for the insecurity
that derives from the lack of direct involvement in productivity by building homogeneous organizations in
which trust levels are high. In the corporation she studied this meant hiring men of Scottish and Irish background who wore similar hairstyles, identical suits,
shirts, and ties—all of which symbolized similar attitudes and a willingness to trust one another.

This demand for homogeneity had a punitive effect on women. The men reported fear of women and inability to communicate with them or to understand how they think. Even women from the same social class could never become "one of the boys." As a result, women were allowed to enter management only in small numbers; even those who succeeded were often clustered in particular departments, such as advertising, in which they were perceived to be less threatening and from which they could rarely compete for top management positions.[40] Women professionals at the turn of the century lacked the advantages of these recent insights. Yet the reasons for their marginality have endured.

## EPILOGUE

Experiences of the first few generations of women professionals firmly established their ability to succeed in graduate school and professional practice; yet women continued to participate with curtailed opportunity and faced both overt and subtle forms of discrimination. The factors related to the creation and distribution of expert knowledge—the overreliance on merit and service as avenues to professional success, the inability to create continuous progeny, and the tendency of experts to recruit colleagues similar to themselves—have remained firmly in place and have helped shape the asymmetry of male and female professional experience up to the present.

This does not mean that the situation for women professionals has remained static. Clearly, the historical context in which any generation of women comes of age changes over time. The factors we have discussed have remained constant, but have been affected by other societal changes. The state of the economy, the political climate, and demographic changes all contributed to the expansion or contraction of women in the professions in different periods.

The fairly positive climate for women during the Progressive period, culminating in the adoption of women's suffrage, declined in the 1920s when the ascendance of antireform politics curtailed the effectiveness of agencies such as the Children's Bureau, which had served as a base for so many women professionals.[41] During the Great Depression the argument for the family wage was reintroduced with new vigor, and there was an insistence that women leave the labor force to make room for men in a scarce job market. At the same time, the New Deal opened some high-level opportunities for a small group of women leaders in the federal government. Not until World War II brought a serious shortage of manpower were women actively recruited into the labor market. Even that success was short-lived when returning veterans demanded that special places be made available for them in schools and the professions. Special treatment for veterans, combined with a grand scale move to the suburbs and a new emphasis on child-centered family life, encouraged women to see homemaking as their career.[42] Although the numbers of college-educated women rose in the 1950s, quotas in medical schools and other professional schools contracted.[43]

The emergence of an expanding economy in the 1960s and the development of a strong women's movement that spearheaded both legislative and court battles in the 1970s helped open new opportunities for women. For the first time since 1920, women appeared in graduate and professional schools in significant numbers. As graduates entered fields where women had never before been employed, there was a growing realization that more women were in the labor market to stay—and would not leave as soon as they married or had children.

However encouraging the opening of law, medical, dental, and engineering schools to women might seem, there is little evidence thus far that the structure of professional life has been significantly modified.[44] The professions continue to be hierarchical with the few difficult-to-reach places at the top reserved for the traditional leadership. Few women are deans of medical or law or business schools, and the number of female tenured faculty at graduate research institutions remains small.

To bring about change, both women and men must recognize that historically merit and service have had different meanings for their respective groups. For able men, the ideology of merit and service has provided access to additional prestige and reward. For women, this ideology has too often been invoked to legitimize their entrance and mere presence in jealously guarded professional precincts rather than to serve as an avenue to higher positions. Recent efforts at creating female networks, professional caucuses, and watchdog committees are laudable. But in the absence of available senior positions, women still need to learn how to penetrate the structures that will give them appropriate openings for professional advancement.

Commitment to superperformance and exceptional achievement has put special burdens on young women's private lives. Women must continue to worry about the integration of professional achievement with marriage, and especially with the rearing of children, in ways that men rarely do. Married women always stand at risk of punishment for success as well as for failure. Continuing social pressures urge them not to exceed their husbands in prestige or income and to assume principal responsibility for home management and child care. No amount of personal resolution, however imaginative, is likely to replace their need for political alliances that can produce social responses to these issues.

MARGINALITY WORKS IN INSIDIOUS WAYS. WHEN WOMEN have to use significant energy to justify and guard hard-won gains instead of applying their creative capacities to more productive uses, they lose out. At its worst, marginality forces women into competition with other disadvantaged groups for scarce entry-level places. It was especially ironic that when recent affirmative action laws finally opened new possibilities for formerly excluded sectors of the society, women and minority groups often found themselves competing for a few places in an over-expanded market. Only the existence of a strong political consciousness, fostered by the women's movement and the civil rights movement among minorities, can enable these new pioneers to understand the political structures they have entered and to muster the necessary power to participate in the professions on equal terms.

At best, the historical experience of existing on the margins will enable these groups to bring a critical stance to professional life, forcing a much needed reconsideration of its values and social structure.

Works and paper collections frequently cited have been identified by the following abbreviations.

AH Papers  Alice Hamilton Papers, Schlesinger Library, Radcliffe College, Cambridge, Massachusetts.

*AMS  American Men of Science.* Edited by J. McKeen Cattell and Jaques Cattell. New York: Science Press, 1938.

BCR Papers  Bertha C. Reynolds Papers, Sophia Smith Collection, Smith College, Northampton, Massachusetts.

DRM Papers  Dorothy Reed Mendenhall Papers, Sophia Smith Collection, Smith College, Northampton, Massachusetts.

FRS Papers  Florence R. Sabin Papers, Sophia Smith Collection.

MCJ Papers  Mary C. Jarrett Papers, Sophia Smith Collection.

MHCL/A  Mount Holyoke College Library, Archives, Mount Holyoke College, South Hadley, Massachusetts.

MvK Papers  Mary van Kleeck Papers, Sophia Smith Collection, Smith College, Northampton, Massachusetts.

*NAW  Notable American Women.* Edited by Edward T. James, Janet Wilson James, and Paul S. Boyer. 3 vols. Cambridge: Harvard University Press, 1971.

*NAW:MP  Notable American Women: The Modern Period.* Edited by Barbara Sicherman and Carol Hurd Green. Cambridge: Harvard University Press, 1980.

## One. The Context of Professionalization

1. One of the benefits of recent feminist scholarship has been the increasing attention paid to the history of women's higher education and the professions. See for example, Rosalind Rosenberg, *Beyond Separate Spheres: Intellectual Roots of Modern Feminism* (New Haven: Yale University Press, 1982); Nancy Cott, *Bonds of Womanhood: Women's Sphere in New England, 1780–1835* (New Haven: Yale University Press, 1977); Margaret W. Rossiter, *Women Scientists in America: Struggles and Strategies to 1940* (Baltimore: Johns Hopkins University Press, 1982); Joan J. Brumberg and Nancy Tomes, "Women in the Professions: A Research Agenda for American Historians," *Reviews in American History* 10 ( June 1982) : 275–296; Helen L. Horowitz, *Alma Mater: Design and Experience in the Women's Colleges from Their Nineteenth-Century Beginnings to the 1930s* (New York: Alfred A. Knopf, 1984); Patricia M. Hummer, *The Decade of Elusive Promise: Professional Women in the United States, 1920–1930* (Ann Arbor, Mich.: UMI Research Press, 1979); Barbara Harris, *Beyond Her Sphere: Women and Professions in American History* (Westport, Conn.: Greenwood Press, 1978); Barbara Solomon, *In the Company of Educated Women* (New Haven: Yale University Press, 1985); Regina Markell Morantz-Sanchez, *Sympathy and Science: Women Physicians in American Medicine* (New York: Oxford University Press, 1985).

2. Women's experience is still apt to be quite different from that of their male counterparts, especially in terms of rewards, career paths, rates of promotion, etc. See, for example, Helen Astin, *The Woman Doctorate in America* (New York: Russell Sage Foundation, 1969); Caroline Bird, *Born Female: The High Cost of Keeping Women Down* (New York: D. McKay, 1968); Cynthia Fuchs Epstein, *Woman's Place: Options and Limits in Professional Careers* (Berkeley: University of California Press,

1970); Ruth Kundsin, ed., *Successful Women in the Sciences: An Analysis of Determinants* (New York: Morrow, 1973); Jacqueline Mattfield and Carol Van Aken, eds., *Women and the Scientific Professions* (Cambridge: Harvard University Press, 1965); Brumberg and Tomes, "Women in the Professions"; Florence Howe, "Three Missions of Higher Education for Women: Vocation, Freedom, Knowledge," *Liberal Education* 66 (Fall 1980); Patricia G. Bourne and Norma Juliet Wikler, "Commitment and the Cultural Mandate," in *Women and Work,* ed. Rachel Kahn-Hut, Arlene Kaplan Daniels, and Richard Colvard (New York: Oxford University Press, 1982), 111–122. For a comprehensive review of the literature, see Londa Scheibinger, "Gender and Science," Paper delivered at the Conference on Gender, Technology, and Education, Bellagio Study and Conference Center, Bellagio, Italy, October 1985, esp. 19 for figures on differential rewards.

3. Dorothy Reed Mendenhall, Unpublished Autobiography (1886–1953), fldr. F, DRM Papers.

4. Ibid.

5. S. Josephine Baker, *Fighting for Life* (New York: Macmillan, 1939), 89.

6. Several important interpretations of the professionalization process are: Magali S. Larson, *The Rise of Professionalism* (Berkeley: University of California Press, 1977); J. A. Jackson, ed., *Professions and Professionalization* (Cambridge: Cambridge University Press, 1970); Burton Bledstein, *The Culture of Professionalism: The Middle Class and the Development of Higher Education in America* (New York: W. W. Norton, 1976), esp. chap. 3. All of these books are principally focused on the experience of men. For an impressive recent study that focuses on a female profession see John H. Ehrenreich, *The Altruistic Imagination: A History of Social Work and Social Policy in the United States* (Ithaca: Cornell University Press, 1985), which examines issues of professionalization.

7. See, for example, John Rousmaniere, "Cultural Hybrid in the Slums: The College Woman and the Settlement House, 1889–1894," *American Quarterly* (Spring 1970): 45–66; Sheila M. Rothman, *Women's Proper Place: A History of Changing Ideals and Practices, 1870 to the Present* (New York: Basic Books, 1978), chap. 3; Joyce Antler, "'After College, What?': New Graduates and the Family Claim," *American Quarterly* 32 (Fall 1980): 409–434.

8. Horowitz, *Alma Mater,* gives an excellent history of the women's colleges and their increasing emphasis on intellectual development.

9. Mendenhall, Unpublished Autobiography, fldr. E, DRM Papers.

10. Quoted in Edith Finch, *Carey Thomas of Bryn Mawr* (New York: Harper, 1947), 92.

11. Alice Hamilton to Agnes Hamilton, 12 September 1896, reprinted in Barbara Sicherman, *Alice Hamilton: A Life in Letters* (Cambridge: Harvard University Press, 1984), 103.

12. Quoted in Joyce Antler, "Was She a Good Mother?" in *Women and the Social Structure,* ed. Barbara Harris and Jo Ann McNamara (Durham, N.C.: Duke University Press, 1984), 57. A significant minority of female physicians, about one-third, married by the 1920s and 1930s, when marriage rates for college graduates began to rise generally; the majority of these continued to practice. See Hummer, *Elusive Promise,* 38.

13. In the 1970s, several important historical studies delineated the nature and extent of prejudice in the professions. See, for example, Gerald Auerbach, *Unequal Justice* (New York: Oxford University Press, 1976); Bledstein, *Culture of Professionalism;* Marcia G. Synott, *The Half-Opened Door: Discrimination and Admissions at Harvard, Yale, and Princeton, 1900–1970* (Westport, Conn.: Greenwood Press, 1979); Mary Roth Walsh, *Doctors Wanted: No Women Need Apply* (New Haven: Yale University Press, 1977).

14. See William Leach, *True Love and Perfect Union: The Feminist Reform of Sex and Society* (New York: Basic Books, 1980), chap. 9, for an excellent discussion of the public definition of women as consumers of commodities; also see, Christopher Lasch, "Life in the Therapeutic State," *New York Review of Books* 12 (June 1980): 24–32; Carroll Smith-Rosenberg and Charles Rosenberg, "The Female Animal: Medical and Biological Views of Woman and Her Role in Nineteenth Century America," *Journal of American History* 60 (1973): 332–356.

15. Larson, *Rise of Professionalism*, 63; Bledstein, *Culture of Professionalism*, chap. 3; Gerald E. Markowitz and David K. Posner, "Doctors in Crisis: A Study of the Use of Medical Education Reform to Establish Modern Professional Elitism in Medicine," *American Quarterly* 25 (March 1973): 83–107.

16. Talcott Parsons, *The Social System* (Glencoe, Ill.: Free Press, 1951); Bledstein, *Culture of Professionalism*, chap. 3; H. Jamous and B. Peloille, "Professions or Self-Perpetuating Systems: Change in the French University Hospital System," in Jackson, *Professions and Professionalization*, 111–152; Terrence Johnson, *Professions and Power* (London: Macmillan, 1972).

17. Morantz, *Sympathy and Science*, 261.

18. Christopher Lasch, *Haven in a Heartless World: The Family Besieged* (New York: Basic Books, 1977).

19. Susan Carter, "Academic Women Revisited: An Empirical Study of Changing Patterns in Women's Employment as College and University Faculty, 1890–1963," *Journal of Social History*, 14 (Summer 1981): 686.

20. Larson, *Rise of Professionalism*, 32–33.

Two. Professional Scholars in Isolated Splendor

1. Emilie J. Hutchinson, *Women and the Ph.D.* (Greensboro, N.C.: North Carolina College for Women, 1930), 2. For a comparative approach, see Patricia M. Hummer, *The Decade*

*of Elusive Promise: Professional Women in the United States, 1920–1930* (Ann Arbor, Mich.: UMI Research Press, 1979), which offers much statistical material as well as a comparison of physicians, lawyers, and doctoral recipients. Barbara Solomon's comprehensive study of women in higher education, *In the Company of Educated women* (New Haven: Yale University Press, 1985), chaps. 8, 11, describes the debate over women's postgraduate employment and further training.

2. Susan Carter, "Academic Women Revisited: An Empirical Study of Changing Patterns in Women's Employment as College and University Faculty, 1890–1963," *Journal of Social History* 14 (Summer 1981): 615–697, esp. 684, 687.

3. Thomas Woody, *A History of Women's Higher Education in the United States* (New York: Lancaster Press, 1929), 2: 327–329. For a study of historians see Kathleen Kish Sklar, "American Female Historians in Context, 1770–1930," *Feminist Studies* (Fall 1975): 171–184, esp. 179–180. According to Carter's figures, at the women's four-year colleges, over 70 percent of the faculty were female during the first four decades of the twentieth century. At the private coeducational institutions, women comprised less than 20 percent of the faculty during the same period and were employed in even smaller numbers at the land grant institutions. Teachers colleges and normal schools were the other places where women were found in substantial numbers. See Carter, "Academic Women Revisited," 680.

4. For a discussion of the early ideals of Mary Lyon, see Tiziana Rota, "'Christian Servants of Society': Towards an Understanding of Mary Lyon and Mount Holyoke," Paper presented at the New England Historical Association Meeting, Holy Cross College, Worcester, Mass., 17 April 1982; also see Elizabeth Alden Green, *Mary Lyon and Mount Holyoke: Opening the Gates* (Hanover, N.H.: University Press of New England, 1979). An important recent book by Helen L. Horo-

witz, *Alma Mater: Design and Experience in the Women's Colleges from Their Nineteenth-Century Beginnings to the 1930s* (New York: Alfred A. Knopf, 1984), discusses the earliest conceptions of the Seven Sisters and their evolution through the 1930s. See chap. 1 for a discussion of Mary Lyon's seminary idea. For an examination of English developments in higher education in the late nineteenth and early twentieth centuries, see Martha Vicinus, *Independent Women: Work and Community for Single women, 1850–1920* (Chicago: University of Chicago Press, 1985), esp. chap. 4, 121–162.

5. Arthur Cole, *A Hundred Years of Mount Holyoke College* (New Haven: Yale University Press, 1940), gives the most complete narrative account. For a comparative discussion of Wellesley, see Patricia Ann Palmieri, "In Adamless Eden: A Social Portrait of the Academic Community at Wellesley College, 1875–1920," Ph.D. diss., Harvard University, 1981, chap. 1; also Horowitz, *Alma Mater,* part 3, esp. chap. 14; see Joyce Antler's perceptive essay on women's options at Wellesley, "'After College, What?': New Graduates and the Family Claim," *American Quarterly* 32 (Fall 1980): 409–434.

6. See "Woolley" in *NAW,* 660–663. A full-length biography emphasizes the relationship with Jeanette Marks; see Anna Mary Wells, *Miss Marks and Miss Woolley* (Boston: Houghton Mifflin, 1978). Also see Mary E. Woolley Papers, MHCL/A.

7. Viola Barnes, *Mount Holyoke in the Twentieth Century, 1971–72,* Oral History Interviews, transcripts, MHCL/A. See also Horowitz, *Alma Mater,* 223–232.

8. Barnes, *Mount Holyoke,* MHCL/A.

9. Mount Holyoke College, President, Report 1905, 6–7, MHCL/A.

10. Ibid., 7.

11. Laurence Veysey, *The Emergence of the American University* (Chicago: University of Chicago Press, 1965), 175–176.

An analogous upgrading of standards also occurred in other colleges including Catholic schools. See, for example, Sister Maria Concepta, *The Making of a Sister Teacher* (Notre Dame: University of Notre Dame Press, 1965), esp. chap. 4.

12. Woody, *Women's Education,* 335, reported that in 1920, of thirteen women's colleges surveyed, one school absolutely forbade employment of married women; four reported that it was not their custom to have married women on the faculty; seven had no teachers with living husbands at the time of the inquiry; and only five reported that about 8 percent of their female faculty were married. Using census figures, Hummer estimates that by the 1920s and 1930s, 11 percent of women college teachers were married, but that number far exceeds the estimates at Mount Holyoke College where it was very rare. See Hummer, *Elusive Promise,* 104–105. Margaret Judson, who entered Mount Holyoke in 1918, writes in her recent memoir of one married woman who taught English literature at the college. See Margaret Judson, *Breaking the Barrier* (New Brunswick, N.J.: Rutgers University Press, 1984), 21.

13. Barnes, *Mount Holyoke,* MHCL/A.

14. See, for example, Virginia G. Drachman, *Hospital with a Heart: Women Doctors and the Paradox of Separatism at the New England Hospital* (Ithaca: Cornell University Press, 1984).

15. Barnes, *Mount Holyoke,* MHCL/A.

16. Mount Holyoke College, *The Catalogue, 1910,* MHCL/A, was typical of most of the early years. Of eighteen full professors, three were male; there were no male associate professors but a few assistant professors and lecturers on short-term appointments; also, Viola Barnes recalled, "The men were in a way gadflies; they didn't have much of a chance at regular participation. Often times Miss Woolley wouldn't even recognize them when they showed they wanted to get up to speak." See Barnes, *Mount Holyoke,* MHCL/A; also Wells, *Miss Marks and Miss Woolley,* 76, 86–87. A similar phenome-

non occurred at several other women's colleges. See, for example, Alice Payne Hackett, *Wellesley: Part of the American Story* (New York: E. P. Dutton, 1949), 85, 143–144. Horowitz's book is an elaborate comparison of the educational philosophies of the Seven Sisters. She uses architectural history to discern much about their educational philosophies. pointing out, for example, that in a number of colleges the women were forced to live on campus and supervise the students, while the men lived off campus and received larger salaries. See Horowitz, *Alma Mater,* esp. chap. 12.

17. Well indicates that the favoritism shown by Miss Woolley to her special friend, Jeanette Marks, was an ongoing irritant that surfaced during the struggle over Woolley's successor. See Wells, *Miss Marks and Miss Woolley,* 226–227.

18. Barnes, *Mount Holyoke,* MHCL/A.

19. Wells, *Miss Marks and Miss Woolley,* 96–97.

20. Mary E. Woolley's Inauguration Address in "The Inauguration Number," *The Mount Holyoke* 15 (May 1901): 12, MHCL/A.

21. Helen Miller Gould to Mary Woolley, 16 May 1903, Mary E. Woolley Papers, MHCL/A.

22. Mary E. Woolley to Helen Miller Gould, June 1903, Mary E. Woolley Papers, MHCL/A.

23. Ellen Deborah Ellis, *Mount Holyoke in the Twentieth Century, 1971–72,* Oral History Interviews, transcripts, MHCL/A.

24. For a good discussion of how home economics fared in various types of institutions, see Joyce Antler, "Culture, Service, and Work: Changing Ideals of Higher Education for Women," in *The Undergraduate Woman: Issues in Educational Equity,* ed. Pamela J. Perun (Lexington, Mass.: D. C. Heath, 1982), 26–28.

25. Mount Holyoke College, President, Report 1919–1920, 6, MHCL/A.

26. Ibid., 8.

27. Ibid., 20.

28. Nellie Neilson, "A Generation of History at Mount Holyoke," *Mount Holyoke Alumnae Quarterly* (May 1939): 9.

29. Obituary, Elizabeth Prentiss, 1922, faculty biographical files, MHCL/A.

30. Neilson, "Generation of History," 9.

31. See "Neilson" in *NAW;* "Putnam" in *NAW:MP.*

32. For a sense of their place in English historiography, see Margaret Hastings and Elisabeth G. Kimball, "Two Distinguished Medievalists—Nellie Neilson and Bertha Putnam," *Journal of British Studies* 18 (Spring 1979): 142–159.

33. Norma Adams, "Nellie Neilson, 1873–1947," *Mount Holyoke Alumnae Quarterly* (February 1948): 154.

34. Laurence Veysey, "The Plural Organized World of the Humanities," in *The Organization of Knowledge in Modern America, 1860–1920,* ed. Alexandra Oleson and John Voss (Baltimore: Johns Hopkins University Press, 1976), 51–57. The Berkshire Historical Association was a very important organization for young women historians. Beginning in 1928, women historians from New England, New York, and New Jersey met annually in the spring to hike in the Berkshires and to discuss their research as well as to support each other as women in a male profession. See Judson, *Breaking the Barrier,* 77–87, for a personal remembrance of this vital group.

35. "Neilson" in *NAW.*

36. Obituary, Nellie Neilson, *London Times,* February 1960, faculty biographical files, MHCL/A.

37. Ibid.

38. Barnes, *Mount Holyoke,* MHCL/A.

39. Jessie M. Tatlock and Alice C. Cramer, with appendix by Nellie Neilson, "The Teaching at Mount Holyoke, 1837–1937," in *Alumnae Association of Mount Holyoke College: 100 Year Biographical Directory of Mount Holyoke College, 1837–1937* (South Hadley, Mass., 1937), from history department rec-

ords. For a general survey of Mount Holyoke College alumnae, see Sophia Meranski, "A Census of Mount Holyoke College Alumnae," *Mount Holyoke Alumnae Quarterly* (October 1924): 149-159.

40. Mount Holyoke College, President, Report 1908-1909, 5, MHCL/A. In another instance of spreading the mission, Margaret Shove Morriss, a faculty member in the history department from 1908 to 1923, left Mount Holyoke to become the dean of Pembroke College and an active promoter of its expansion within Brown University; see Morriss, faculty biographical files, MHCL/A.

41. Among the most distinguished graduates who went on to successful careers as historians was Margaret A. Judson (Mount Holyoke, A.B. 1922; Radcliffe, A.M. 1923, Ph.D. 1933), who authored several books on English constitutional history, including *The Crisis of the Constitution: An Essay in Constitutional and Political Thought in England, 1603-1645* (New Brunswick, N.J.: Rutgers University Press, 1949). She received a Guggenheim fellowship in 1954-1955. Others include Margaret Hastings (Mount Holyoke, B.A. 1931, M.A. 1932; Bryn Mawr, Ph.D. 1939), author of *The Court of Common Pleas in 15th Century England* (Ithaca: Cornell University Press, 1947) and other works in medieval history, received a Fulbright grant in 1950-1951, a Guggenheim fellowship in 1959-1960, and an American Council of Learned Societies award in 1964-1965; Elisabeth G. Kimball (Mount Holyoke, B.A. 1921; Oxford, M.A. 1925; Yale, Ph.D. 1933) is known for her *Serjeanty Tenure in Medieval England* (New Haven: Yale University Press, 1936).

42. Liva Baker, *I'm Radcliffe, Fly Me! The Seven Sisters and the Future of Women's Education* (New York: Macmillan, 1976), offers a critical perspective of the single-sex institutions for their failure to take leadership on any intellectual or political questions about women. Horowitz's *Alma Mater* is a more

scholarly attempt to look at the changing conception of the purpose of women's education and the way that conception influenced the design and direction of the women's colleges.

43. Neilson, Generation of History," 9.

44. William Stubbs, *The Constitutional History of England* (Oxford: Clarendon Press, 1874), 3–4, quoted in Neilson, "Generation of History," 9; Judson, in her memoir, points out that a disproportionate number of women at the Berkshire Historical Association were working in British history. For a good bibliography of the work of these women see Judson, *Breaking the Barrier,* 82–84.

45. Evelyn Fox Keller, "Gender and Science," *Psychoanalysis and Contemporary Thought* 1 (1978):409–433.

46. M. Carey Thomas, "Present Tendencies in Women's Colleges and University Education," *Educational Review* 35 (January 1908):81–82, called for women's colleges to develop doctoral programs as a high priority.

47. Sklar, "American Female Historians," 179–180; for an insightful discussion of women academics at undergraduate colleges see Charles H. Page, *50 Years in the Sociological Enterprise: A Lucky Journey* (Amherst: University of Massachusetts Press, 1982), 114–117.

48. Mount Holyoke College, President, Report 1920–1923, 22, MHCL/A.

49. For a good discussion of the conflicting goals of women's colleges see Antler, "Changing Ideals," 15–41, esp. 29–32; see also Horowitz, *Alma Mater,* 304, for a discussion of changes at Mount Holyoke College.

50. There is an ongoing debate on the marriage rates of early college graduates. The most recent studies suggest that even in the early decades of the twentieth century the majority of college women did marry, but later in life and in fewer numbers than those who received less education. See Solomon, *Educated Women,* 119–122; Mabel Newcomer, *A Century of*

*Higher Education for American Women* (New York: Harper and Row, 1959), 212–213; Roberta Frankfort, *Collegiate Women: Domesticity and Career in Turn-of-the-Century America* (New York: New York University Press, 1977), 56–57, 112–113.

51. "The Confessions of a Woman Professor," *The Independent* 55 (1903):955.

52. Ibid.

53. Neilson, "Generation of History," 10.

54. Edith Finch, *Carey Thomas of Bryn Mawr* (New York: Harper, 1947), 92.

55. Ibid., 52.

56. Carey Thomas to Millicent Carey McIntosh, 22 May 1932, reprinted in *The Making of a Feminist: Early Journals and Letters of M. Carey Thomas,* ed. Marjorie Housepian Dobkin (Kent, Ohio: Kent State University Press, 1979), xiv.

57. Ibid., xv.

58. Christopher Lasch, "Life in the Therapeutic State," *New York Review of Books,* 12 June 1980, 25, points out that historically feminists have chosen to attack the family rather than address the conflicts between men and women; see also, Bernice Fischer, "The Wise Old Men and the New Women: Christopher Lasch Besieged," *History of Education Quarterly,* Spring 1979, 125–141, approvingly calls attention to Lasch's insight on this point.

59. Mary Woolley was not alone in this. Carey Thomas also defended college as a training ground for educated mothers, while holding other aspirations for her students. See Sheila Rothman, *Woman's Proper Place* (New York: Basic Books, 1978), 107.

60. Wells, *Miss Marks and Miss Woolley,* chap. 11, esp. 231. President Ham also began to change the composition of the faculty. In the early 1940s Viola Barnes was chair of the history department. She was about to offer a position to Margaret Judson, a distinguished alumna who was teaching at

New Jersey College for Women. Ham rejected this recommendation because he felt there were too many older women at the college and that any new appointment should go to a younger man. Judson was then in her early forties. See Judson, *Breaking the Barrier*, 75–76; also, Horowitz, *Alma Mater*, 304.

61. Estelle Freedman, "Separatism as Strategy: Female Institution Building and American Feminism, 1870–1930," *Feminist Studies* 5 (Fall 1979): 512–529. Patricia Palmieri and Rosalind Rosenberg have both recently argued that separatism had peaked in the colleges by the turn of the century. The experience of Mount Holyoke reveals that for women with professional aspirations, the first quarter of the twentieth century was the most important. The reassertion of the private sphere and the claims it made on women's lives surface in a significant way in the 1930s; see papers delivered at a panel titled "Two Traditions: Coeducation and Separate Education for Women," Sesquicentennial Symposium, Mount Holyoke College, 21 September 1984. See also Vicinus, *Independent Women, passim*.

62. Drachman, *Hospital*, 61.

63. This phenomenon was true in almost all the women's colleges. Thomas Mendenhall, in his 1966 president's report, presented a portrait of the Smith faculty: "Two out of three chances are that he is a man and probably married with children." Mendenhall went on to indicate that this represented a marked shift in the gender composition of the faculty:

A half-century ago when higher education was expanding more slowly and there were fewer opportunities for the woman professor, the percentage of women on the Smith faculty rose as high as 75% in 1910. This represented an imbalance of a sort. . . . Since World War II the percentage (which was still at 63% [female] in 1939) has declined steadily until it stands at 35% this year. . . . These days a woman may teach at a steadily increasing number of institutions besides Smith; yet that is no excuse for Smith not to halt this decline in its own best interests. (Report of the President, Smith College Archives, Smith College, Northampton, Mass., 1966, 4–7)

### Three. Motherhood and Medicine

1. Although there were a number of female medical colleges at this time, they were of mixed quality. This is not surprising since it was rare for any medical school in the country to require a college education or training in the sciences. Among the more prestigious schools, Harvard accepted no women and Cornell agreed to accept a few in return for a $25,000 endowment. The biggest breakthrough came when Mary E. Garrett donated over $300,000 to the $500,000 endowment campaign and thereby compelled Johns Hopkins to open that school with equal terms for women and men. One distinguished pathologist resigned in protest. See Mary Roth Walsh, *Doctors Wanted: No Women Need Apply* (New Haven: Yale University Press, 1977), 169, 176–177; also see table on female enrollment, 183; Simon Flexner and James Thomas Flexner, *William Henry Walsh and the Heroic Age of American Medicine* (New York: Viking Press, 1941), 215–217.

2. For a study of the separatist tradition in women's medicine, see Virginia G. Drachman, *Hospital with a Heart: Women Doctors and the Paradox of Separatism at the New England Hospital* (Ithaca: Cornell University Press, 1984); Walsh, *Doctors Wanted,* chap. 3, also gives an excellent background of the separatist tradition.

3. *New York Times,* 1 August 1964; Dorothy Reed Mendenhall, Unpublished Autobiography (1886–1953), DRM Papers. Much of the material on Mendenhall in this chapter was first published in Miriam Slater and Penina Glazer, "Natural and Sacred Professions: Motherhood and Medicine

in America," in *Marriage and Society: Studies in the Social History of Marriage,* ed. E. B. Outhwaite (London: Europa Publications Limited, 1981), chap. 11, 256–280. See also Regina Markell Morantz-Sanchez, *Sympathy and Science: Women Physicians in American Medicine* (New York: Oxford University Press, 1985).

4. Anne Walter Fearn, *My Days of Strength: An American Woman Doctor's Forty Years in China* (New York: Macmillan, 1939), chap. 1; Walsh, *Doctors Wanted,* 72–73, 178–180. Both discuss the importance of the women's medical colleges, founded between 1848 and 1895, in the face of bitter opposition from the male medical establishment. Once small numbers of women were accepted at the male-controlled medical schools (especially Johns Hopkins, Cornell, and Tufts), women erroneously assumed that their schools had outlived their purpose. In the early part of the twentieth century, all but Women's Medical College of Pennsylvania closed their doors.

5. Reed was thirty-two years old; Fearn was twenty-nine.

6. Magali Larson, *The Rise of Professionalism: A Sociological Analysis* (Berkeley: University of California Press, 1977); Oswald Hall, "Stages in a Professional Career," in *Professionalization,* ed. Howard M. Vollmer and Donald L. Mills (Englewood Cliffs, N.J.: Prentice Hall, 1966), 91–92; an important addition to the history of medicine is Paul Starr, *The Social Transformation of American Medicine* (New York: Basic Books, 1982); Eliot Friedson, *The Profession of Medicine* (New York: Dodd, Mead, 1972), 82–84, 359–382, shows that all of these changes were not as totally value free as the profession often presented them.

7. Rosemary Stevens, *Medicine and the Public Interest* (New Haven: Yale University Press, 1971).

8. Barbara Ehrenreich and Deirdre English, *For Her Own Good: One Hundred Fifty Years of the Experts' Advice to Women* (Garden City, N.J.: Doubleday, 1978), 56–57. See also Larson,

*Rise of Professionalism,* 22, for an excellent discussion of the doctor-patient relationship. Larson's analysis points to the "extra professional sources of credibility and legitimation" that were so important for physicians. We would argue further that female physicians had special disadvantages in drawing on these sources of credibility.

9. Drachman, *Hospital,* chap. 1; see also Ehrenreich and English, *For Her Own Good,* 84–88; Walsh, *Doctors Wanted,* chap. 4.

10. Mendenhall, Unpublished Autobiography, fldr. A, DRM Papers.

11. Ibid., fldr. F.

12. Ibid., fldr. D.

13. Ibid.; see also William G. Rothstein, *American Physicians in the Nineteenth Century: From Sects to Science* (Baltimore: Johns Hopkins University Press, 1972), 290–291. The earlier medical schools offered very poor science education, no research, and little clinical instruction. Not until after the Civil War did Harvard Medical School even acquire microscopes or stethoscopes. The new education placed strong premium on science and laboratory instruction and the bedside method of clinical instruction. A report by Abraham Flexner became very important in the early twentieth century in forcing other schools to move to scientific, research-based education and to close down the small proprietary schools. See Abraham Flexner, *Medical Education in the United States and Canada* (1910; reprint, New York: Carnegie Foundation, 1972).

14. Mendenhall, Unpublished Autobiography, fldr. G, DRM Papers.

15. Ibid.

16. Emily Blackwell, "Women in the Regular Medical Profession," Address delivered 26 March 1878, *Report of the Association for the Advancement of the Medical Education of Women* (New York, 1878), 10.

See, for example, discussion of women's health in Sheila M. Rothman, *Woman's Proper Place: A History of Changing Ideals and Practices, 1870 to the Present* (New York: Basic Books, 1978), 30-32.

17. Mendenhall, Unpublished Autobiography, fldr. F, DRM Papers.

18. S. Josephine Baker, *Fighting for Life* (New York: Macmillan, 1939).

19. Mendenhall, Unpublished Autobiography, fldr. F, DRM Papers.

20. Emily Dunning Barringer, *Bowery to Bellevue: The Story of New York's First Woman Ambulance Driver* (New York: W. W. Norton, 1950), 115.

21. Ibid., 105-106.

22. Ibid., 132, 175, 178, 199.

23. The period was noted for its production of advice manuals aimed at women of this class, frequently authored by male doctors, which warned of the dangers of strenuous activity. Women professionals clearly broke with this tradition and flouted these dicta. Jill Conway, "Stereotypes of Femininity in a Theory of Sexual Evolution," in *Suffer and Be Still,* ed. Martha Vicinus (Bloomington, Ind.: University of Indiana Press, 1973), 140-154, documents the theories concerning the belief in the innate differences between men and women; Barbara J. Harris, *Beyond Her Sphere: Women and the Professions in American History* (Westport, Conn.: Greenwood Press, 1978), chap. 2, contains a detailed summary of the cult of domesticity in the late-nineteenth-century United States; see Rothman, *Woman's Proper Place,* 23-26.

24. Baker, *Fighting for Life,* 64-65.

25. Barringer, *Bowery to Bellevue,* 97ff.

26. Ibid., 23.

27. In her memoirs Mendenhall comments that she did not like Miss Wald (Lillian Wald, the settlement house leader) because the latter overworked her staff. She goes on to say that

"women do not stand authority well," and "women in positions over other women tend to become tyrants." In Mendenhall, Unpublished Autobiography, fldr. F, DRM Papers.

28. Ibid.

29. Ibid.

30. Edith Finch, *Carey Thomas of Bryn Mawr* (New York: Harper, 1947), describes these friendships in great detail.

31. Mendenhall, Unpublished Autobiography, fldr. F, DRM Papers.

32. Ibid.

33. Ibid.

34. Ibid.

35. Ibid., fldr. E.

36. Ibid.

37. They were not the only ones who believed that at least coeducation had been assured. This conviction resulted in the closing of almost all the women's medical colleges only to find that women applicants were not given equal consideration and that their numbers were generally kept to a quota of 5 percent. Harvard University did not admit women to its medical school until after the Second World War, despite repeated efforts to challenge their policy. See Walsh, *Doctors Wanted,* chap. 6, also tables on 193 and 245.

38. Barringer, *Bowery to Bellevue,* 67–68.

39. Mendenhall, Unpublished Autobiography, fldr. F, DRM Papers.

40. Ibid.

41. Ibid., fldr. G.

42. Ibid., fldr. H.

43. Ibid., fldr. F.

44. Ibid.

45. Ibid.

46. Ibid., fldr. G.

47. Ibid., fldr. I.

48. Ibid.

49. Ibid., fldr. G.
50. Ibid., fldr. H.
51. Ibid.
52. Ibid.
53. Ehrenreich and English, *For Her Own Good*, 86–87.
54. Mendenhall, Unpublished Autobiography, fldr. I, DRM Papers. No copy of the paper is left in the collection of Reed's published work in the Sophia Smith Collection.
55. Ibid.
56. Ibid.
57. Baker, *Fighting for Life*, 138.
58. Ibid.
59. Mendenhall, Unpublished Autobiography, fldr. J, DRM Papers.
60. Ibid., fldr. I.
61. Antifemale acts had a long tradition among the medical associations. See Walsh, *Doctors Wanted*, 25–34, 106–146.
62. Mendenhall, Unpublished Autobiography, fldr. J, DRM Papers.
63. Ibid.
64. Fearn, *Days of Strength*, 104.
65. Ibid., 6.
66. Ibid., 11.
67. Ibid., 12.
68. Ibid.
69. Ibid., 24.
70. Ibid., 103.
71. Ibid., 17–18.
72. Ibid., 18.
73. Ibid., 28.
74. Ibid., 87.
75. Ibid., 95.
76. Ibid., 96.
77. Ibid..

78. Ibid., 102–103.
79. Ibid., 143.
80. Ibid.
81. Ibid., 179–180.
82. Ibid., 216.
83. Ibid.
84. Ibid., 261.
85. Ibid., 263.
86. Larson, *Rise of Professionalism,* 163–166.
87. Ibid., 38–39.
88. Ibid., 40–44. For an analysis of the French case see H. Jamous and B. Peloille, "Changes in the French University Hospital System," in *Professions and Professionalization,* ed. J. A. Jackson (Cambridge: Cambridge University Press, 1970), 111–152. Of course, the concern with altruism should not be understood solely as a defensive legitimizing strategy. We are not arguing that individuals did not vary in the degree of their concern. We are offering a structural analysis of the meaning of altruism in women's professional lives.
89. Mendenhall, Unpublished Autobiography, fldr. H, DRM Papers.
90. Fearn, *Days of Strength,* 95–96, 260–261.
91. Mendenhall, Unpublished Autobiography, fldr. G, DRM Papers.
92. Ibid., fldr. H.
93. Ehrenreich and English, *For Her Own Good,* chap. 4; Carroll Smith-Rosenberg and Charles Rosenberg, "The Female Animal: Medical and Biological Views of Woman and Her Role in Nineteenth Century America," *Journal of American History* 60 (September 1973):332–356; Carroll Smith-Rosenberg, "The Hysterical Woman: Sex Roles and Role Conflict in 19th Century America," *Social Research* 39 (Winter 1972):652–678.
94. For a discussion among early women medical leaders of

the controversy over science versus service, see Regina Morantz, "Feminism, Professionalism, and Germs: A Study on
the Thought of Mary Putnam Jacobi and Elizabeth Blackwell," *American Quarterly* 34 (Winter 1982): 459–478.

## Four. New Opportunities in Science

1. Elinor Bluemel, *Florence Sabin: Colorado Woman of the
Century* (Boulder: University of Colorado Press, 1959); Mary
Day Phelan, *Probing the Unknown: The Story of Dr. Florence
Sabin* (New York: Thomas Y. Crowell Co., 1969); "Sabin" in
*NAW: MP*, 614–617.

2. Alice Hamilton, *Exploring Dangerous Trades* (Boston:
Little, Brown, 1943); also "Hamilton" in *NAW: MP*, 303–306.
An important biography is Barbara Sicherman, *Alice Hamilton: A Life in Letters* (Cambridge: Harvard University Press,
1984).

3. Sally Kohlstedt, "In from the Periphery: American
Women in Science, 1830–1880," *Signs* 4 (August 1978): 90.

4. Ibid., 95; Margaret W. Rossiter, *Women Scientists in
America* (Baltimore: Johns Hopkins University Press, 1982),
19. Several important general histories are William Rothstein,
*American Physicians in the Nineteenth Century* (Baltimore: Johns
Hopkins University Press, 1972); Hugh Hawkins, *Pioneer: A
History of the Johns Hopkins University, 1874–1889* (Ithaca: Cor-
nell University Press, 1960), 21–25, 90; W. Carson Ryan,
*Studies in Early Graduate Education* (New York: Carnegie Foun-
dation, 1939); Paul Starr, *The Social Transformation of American
Medicine* (New York: Basic Books, 1982).

5. Jonathan Cole, *Fair Science: Women in the Scientific Community* (New York: Free Press, 1979), 214.

6. Barbara Reskin, "Scientific Productivity, Sex, and Location in the Institution of Science," *American Journal of Sociology* 83 (March 1978): 1235–1243.

7. This material was first published in Margaret W. Rossiter, "'Women's Work' in Science, 1880–1910," *ISIS* 71 (1980): 381–398; it appears in its most complete form in her book, *Women Scientists*.

8. Deborah Warner, "Women Astronomers," *Natural History* 88 (May 1979): 12–26, esp. 14.

9. In addition to more than twenty female astronomy assistants at Harvard, Rossiter points out that there were twenty-four women in the Dudley Observatory in Albany, twelve at Yerkes Observatory in Washington, D.C., twelve at Mount Wilson in California, and a number scattered in other observatories throughout the country. See Rossiter, "Women's Work," 385.

10. Ibid., 390.

11. Cole, *Fair Science*, 212; Frank Stricker, "Cookbooks and Law Books: The Hidden History of Career Women in Twentieth Century America," *Journal of Social History* 10 (Fall 1976): 1–19, esp. 6–8.

12. Phelan, *Probing the Unknown*, 66–69; Dorothy Reed Mendenhall, Unpublished Autobiography (1886–1953), fldr. E, DRM Papers.

13. Phelan, *Probing the Unknown*, 66–67.

14. See discussion in previous chapter.

15. Phelan, *Probing the Unknown*, 62, 69.

16. Ibid., 77.

17. Ibid., 86; "Sabin" in *AMS*.

18. George W. Corner, *A History of the Rockefeller Institute* (New York: Rockefeller Institute Press, 1964), 238–242; Phelan, *Probing the Unknown*, chap. 17.

19. Mendenhall, Unpublished Autobiography, fldr. F, DRM Papers; "Sabin" in *NAW: MP*, 615.

20. Margaret Mall Vagrales to Elinor Bluemel, 16 September 1955, box 30, FRS Papers.

21. Amy E. MacMahon to Elinor Bluemel, 20 September 1955, box 30, FRS Papers.

22. Dorothy Reed Mendenhall to Elinor Bluemel, 19 September 1955, FRS Papers.

23. Mrs. Edgar Freeman to Elinor Bluemel, 11 September 1955, FRS Papers; Phelan, *Probing the Unknown*, 33.

24. Rossiter, *Women Scientists*, 315; Cole, *Fair Science*, 249.

25. Barbara Kuhn Campbell, *The "Liberated" Woman of 1914* (Ann Arbor, Mich.: UMI Research Press, 1979), chap. 3, esp. 48. She used a sample of all women in *Who's Who of 1914*. Of this group, 57.1 percent of all women in the professions married; also see Rossiter, *Women Scientists*, 140–141.

26. Mary S. Forbe to Elinor Bluemel, 18 September 1955, FRS Papers.

27. Bessie L. Moses to Elinor Bluemel, 6 September 1955, FRS Papers.

28. Dr. Frederic Lewis, Department of Anatomy, Harvard Medical School to Florence Sabin, 1935, FRS Papers.

29. Louise Pearce to Florence Sabin, 1938–1953, FRS Papers.

30. Margaret Rossiter presents some evidence that Sabin tried to influence women scientists to apply for Guggenheim fellowships, although the number of awards to women did not go up during her tenure. Furthermore, she was careful not to lose credibility by advocating the appointment of women. See Rossiter, *Women Scientists*, 274–275; Phelan, *Probing the Unknown*, 129–130.

31. Kate C. Mead to Florence Sabin, 18 July 1938, FRS Papers.

32. Phelan, *Probing the Unknown*, 93, 137.

33. Dr. Thomas R. Rivers to Elinor Bluemel, 15 September 1955, FRS Papers.

34. Ibid.

35. Corner, *Rockefeller*, 56–57. Among the original members were a greater number of Jews and foreigners than could normally be found at a university at that time. The roster in-

cluded such names as Samuel Meltzer, Hideyo Naguchi, and Phoebus Aaron Theodor Bevene.

36. Ibid., 587–595. All figures are derived from Corner, Appendix III, "Role of the Trustees, Scientific Directors, Scientific Staff, and Senior Administrative Staff of the Rockefeller Institute during the Period Covered by This History (50 years)"; also see Simon Flexner, "The Scientific Career for Women," *Scientific Monthly* (August 1921): 103. The 1930s represented a general setback for women professionals. There was a decline in the proportion of women Ph.D.s and a general trend toward increasing inequality in professional life. Cole argues in his study of women in science that first appointments of women and men Ph.D.s were roughly similar, but that the gap widened significantly in each stage of the career cycle thereafter. See Cole, *Fair Science*, 223. Our data show a decided regression in the initial appointments of women as well as in subsequent opportunities.

37. "Pearce," "Lynch," "Wollstein," and "Florence," in *AMS; New York Times*, 12 May 1947, 11 August 1959; Corner, *Rockefeller*, 114, 134, 218–223, 225–227.

38. Several very successful women went from Rockefeller Institute to the University of Colorado, the University of Illinois, and the University of Toronto. The men, of course, had a much greater impact. By the time Flexner retired in 1935, 152 Rockefeller scientists had become associate or full professors in sixty-two professional schools, universities, and colleges. See Corner, *Rockefeller*, 324; also E. Richard Brown, *Rockefeller Medicine Men* (Berkeley: University of California Press, 1972), 324.

39. Cole, *Fair Science*, 229, 237; Margaret Rossiter, "Women Scientists before 1920," *American Scientist* 62 (May–June 1974): 312–323, esp. 318–320.

40. Corner, *Rockefeller*, 226.

41. Ibid., Appendix III.

42. Louise Pearce to Florence Sabin, 20 October 1950, FRS Papers.

43. Ibid., 19 October 1951.

44. Rockefeller Foundation official Frank Blair Hanson, 16 March 1934, quoted in Rossiter, *Women Scientists*, 271.

45. Stanley Cohen, "Foundational Officials and Fellowships," *Minerva* 14 (1976):266.

46. Hamilton, *Exploring*, 97.

47. Ibid.

48. "Tunnicliff," in *AMS*.

49. Emile J. Hutchinson, *Women and the Ph.D.* (Greensboro, N.C.: North Carolina College for Women, 1929), 190; also quoted in Cole, *Fair Science*, 221.

50. Jacques Jork[?] to Mrs. E. Mary East, 8 May 1917, fldr. 461, Ames Family Papers, Sophia Smith Collection, Smith College, Northampton, Mass. When E. Mary East sent out invitations to a number of distinguished scientists to participate on the board of the Massachusetts Birth Control League, which wanted to further research in birth control, one Rockefeller scientist replied, "I am still a little reluctant in permitting the use of my name on letterheads in this movement [birth control] for the reason that in New York too many individuals are engaged in this campaign with whom neither you nor your husband nor I would care to be classified."

51. "Who's Who in Industrial Medicine and Science," typescript, for *Industrial Medicine* (August 1935), fldr. 1D, 21, AH Papers.

52. Hamilton, *Exploring*, 51–52.

53. Ibid., chap. 4.

54. Alice Hamilton to Agnes Hamilton, 23 June 1899, in Sicherman, *Alice Hamilton*, 133.

55. Ibid., 134.

56. Ibid., 114.

57. Ibid., 119.

58. Ibid., 115.

59. Ibid., 122 and *passim.*

60. Ibid., 119.

61. Ibid., 128.

62. See various magazine and newspaper clippings, AH Papers.

63. Hamilton, *Exploring,* 132–133.

64. Corner, *Rockefeller,* 104–105, 241, 470–472; Brown, *Medicine Men,* 120–122 and 129, points out that it was rare for any Rockefeller investigators to examine the relationships between social factors and health. That did not qualify as science. A more mechanistic view of the body fit well the corporate mentality of those funding the research.

65. Hamilton, *Exploring,* 253.

66. David L. Edsall to Alice Hamilton, 27 December 1918, AH Papers.

67. Edsall to Hamilton, 24 January 1919, AH Papers.

68. Alice Hamilton to Edith Hamilton, 11 January 1919, AH Papers.

69. Alice Hamilton to Edith Hamilton, appended to letter of David L. Edsall, 24 January 1919, AH papers.

70. Hamilton, *Exploring,* 252.

71. Ibid., 253.

72. Ester Harney, "A Woman on the Harvard Faculty," *New York Tribune,* 20 April 1919, AH Papers.

73. Alice Hamilton to Clara Landsberg, 6 February 1926, in Sicherman, *Alice Hamilton,* 294.

74. Hamilton, *Exploring,* 267.

75. Harney, "Harvard,"

76. Hamilton, *Exploring,* 268–269.

77. "Hamilton" in *NAW : MP,* 305.

78. See correspondence with Felix Frankfurter, various priests in the Catholic church, defenders and opponents of Alger Hiss, AH Papers.

79. Mendenhall, Unpublished Autobiography, fldr. I, DRM Papers; Mary R. Walsh, *Doctors Wanted: No Women Need Apply* (New Haven: Yale University Press, 1977), chap. 6, 193, 245.

80. Hamilton, *Exploring,* 268.

81. "Goldsmith" in *NAW: MP,* 283-284.

82. "Cori" in *NAW: MP,* 165-167.

83. "Macklin" in *NAW: MP,* 451-452.

84. Magali S. Larson, *The Rise of Professionalism* Berkeley: University of California Press, 1977), 31-34.

85. Cole, *Fair Science,* 219-220.

86. Mendenhall, Unpublished Autobiography, fldr. I, DRM Papers. For an excellent overview of the multifaceted bias against women in science, see Londa Schiebinger, "Gender and Science," paper presented at Bellagio Conference on Gender, Technology, and Education, Bellagio, Italy, October 1985 (forthcoming in *Signs*).

87. Hamilton, *Exploring,* 268.

### Five. The Creation of Psychiatric Social Work

1. Three important histories of social work are John H. Ehrenreich, *The Altruistic Imagination: A History of Social Work and Social Policy in the United States* (Ithaca: Cornell University Press, 1985); Roy Lubove, *The Professional Altruist: The Emergence of Social Work as a Career* (1965; reprint, New York: Atheneumn, 1977); Barbara E. Brand, "The Influence of Higher Education on Sextyping in Three Professions, 1870-1920: Librarianship, Social Work, and Public Health," Ph.D. diss., University of Washington, 1978, esp. 200-236.

2. Ehrenreich, *Altruistic Imagination,* chap. 2, 43-77, for an enlightening account of social work in this period, especially the status problem. Unfortunately, Ehrenreich's book came out too late for us to incorporate it fully in our analysis;

ours was derived independently. We agree with Ehrenreich's rendering on major points concerning psychiatric social work in the 1920s, although he is more interested in the development of the bureaucratic controls of social workers and we put greater emphasis on the importance of gender relationships.

3. "Jarrett" in *NAW: MP*, 377–379; E. E. Southard and Mary C. Jarrett, *The Kingdom of Evils: 100 Case Histories* (New York: Macmillan, 1922).

4. For a brief review of her accomplishments, see William Schwartz, "Bertha Reynolds as Educator," *Catalyst* 11 (1981). Her own account of her life is much more detailed. See Bertha C. Reynolds, "Informal Autobiography," BCR Papers. We wish to thank our former student, Helen Cohen, for calling our attention to the BCR Papers.

5. See, for example, "Report of the Smith College Alumnae Committee on Cooperation with the Training School for Social Work," 19 October 1922, Smith College School for Social Work Records, Smith College Archives, Northampton, Mass. This committee included the following accomplished women who were quite sophisticated about the need for professional credentials:

Anne McClallan Chapin, former acting general secretary of the Children's Aid Association, Northampton, Mass.

Dorothea de Schweinitz, supervisor of guidance and placement, Junior Employment Service of the Board of Public Education of Philadelphia.

Elizabeth Susan Dixon, supervisor of fieldwork in the Graduate School of Social Service Administration, University of Chicago.

Edna Lois Foley, superintendent, Visiting Nurse Association of Chicago.

Annie T. Gerry, Red Cross liaison officer, U.S. Veterans Bureau, District No. 1.

Anne Perry Hincks, executive secretary, Bethesda Society of Boston.

Eleanor Hope Johnson, Hartford School of Religious Pedagogy.

Ellen Jones, member of the staff of Social Service Department of the Boston Psychopath Hospital.

Ora Mabelle Lewis, Social Service Department of Massachusetts General Hospital.

Vivian Betsy Libbery, supervisor of districts, Philadelphia Society for Organizing Charity.

Maude Emma Miner, secretary, New York Probation and Protective Association.

Nellie J. M. Olesen, field agent of Community Service, Inc.

Mary Cynthia Smith, Medical Social Service, Minneapolis.

Jean F. Spahr, president of board of directors of the College Settlement, New York.

Elizabeth H. Webster, associate director, Chicago Council of Social Agencies.

Mary van Kleeck, chairman, director, Industrial Studies Department, Russell Sage Foundation.

6. Abraham Flexner, "Is Social Work a Profession?" in *Proceedings of the Conference on Charities and Corrections, 1915,* (Chicago: 1915), 576–590. For the significance of his work on the medical profession, see, for example, J. H. Means, "Homo Medicum Americanus," in *The Professions in America,* ed. K. S. Lynn (Boston: Houghton Mifflin, 1965), 55–57; also

Mary R. Walsh, *Doctors Wanted: No Women Need Apply* (New Haven: Yale University Press, 1977), 239–240; Paul Starr, *The Social Transformation of American Medicine* (New York: Basic Books, 1982), 118–126.

7. "Revised Program for 42nd Annual Session," *National Conference on Charities and Corrections* 69 (April 1915):17.

8. Flexner, "Is Social Work a Profession?" 586.

9. Ibid., 590.

10. Ibid.

11. Means, "Homo Medicum Americanus," 55–56.

12. Terrence Johnson, *Professions and Power* (London: Macmillan, 1972), chap. 1.

13. Flexner, "Is Social Work a Profession?" 580. In this connection see Judith Long Laws, "Work Aspiration of Women: False Leads and New Starts," in *Women and the Workplace,* ed. M. Blaxall and B. Reagan (Chicago: University of Chicago Press, 1976), 33–49. Laws's modern delineation of the "Myth of the Heroic Male Professional" bears a striking congruence to Flexner's definition of a professional. See esp. 36.

14. Flexner, "Is Social Work a Profession?" 590. In this context, it is instructive to note that two leading historians of social work, Roy Lubove and John Ehrenreich, both use *altruist* in their titles.

15. "Jarrett" in *NAW: MP,* 377–379.

16. Lubove, *Professional Altruist,* 63.

17. Mary C. Jarrett, Curriculum Vitae, MCJ Papers; also, memo, E. E. Southard to Dr. Thomas W. Salmon, June 1919, MCJ Papers.

18. Esther C. Cook, interview by Vida S. Grayson, 22 July 1978, Social Work Archive of the Sophia Smith Collection, Smith College, Northampton, Mass.

19. Ibid.

20. Rose Hahn Dewson, interview by Vida S. Grayson, 22 July 1978, Social Work Archive of the Sophia Smith Collection, Smith College, Northampton, Mass.

21. Cook, interview, 22 July 1978.

22. E. E. Southard, "A Lay Reaction to Psychiatry," *Mental Hygiene* 2 (October 1918) : 5.

23. Ibid.

24. Ibid., 6; also E. E. Southard, "The Training School of Psychiatric Social Work at Smith College," *Mental Hygiene* 2 (October 1918) : 5.

25. Southard, "Lay Reaction to Psychiatry," 6.

26. Ibid.

27. Southard's own work gives a good idea of the state of the field. Much of his scholarship revolved around his interest in classification. He set up categories and encouraged social workers to classify their cases of social maladjustment as follows: "Morbi–Disease," "Errores–Ignorance," "Vitia–Vices and Bad Habits," "Delicta–Crime and Delinquency," "Penuriae–Poverty and Resourcelessness." See, "The Kingdom of Evil, Advantages of an Orderly Approach in Social Case Analysis," *National Conference of Social Work* (1918), 7. Southard did not reject the psychoanalytic model, as many of his contemporary psychiatrists did. But in 1918 he had a very vague approach to this area which he elaborated through one hundred cases in the book he wrote with Mary Jarrett, *The Kingdom of Evils: 100 Case Histories*.

28. Cook, interview, 22 July 1978.

29. Application Form, Smith College School for Social Work Records, Smith College Archives, Northampton, Mass.

30. See "Report of the Smith College Alumnae Committee," 19 October 1922. On Jarrett's role, see W. A. Neilson to Jarrett, 1 November 1922, MCJ Papers; see also an exchange of letters between Christine C. Robb and Miss Lewis concerning Jarrett's original title, Spring 1931, MCJ Papers.

31. Jarrett, Curriculum Vitae, MCJ Papers.

32. Mary C. Jarrett, "Psychiatric Social Work," Careers for Women Series, in *Express* (10 January 1921), MCJ Papers.

33. "Richmond" in *NAM,* 152–154. Richmond was espe-

cially concerned with giving up "wholesale social work" and thought research should be on individual cases that would prevent family disintegration. For a discussion of this see Joyce Antler and Stephen Antler, "Social Policy and the Family: The Progressive Vision," Paper delivered at the Conference on Historical Perspectives on Scientific Study of Fertility in the United States, December 1977, 27–28.

34. Jarrett, "Psychiatric Social Work," MCJ Papers.

35. Ibid.

36. W. A. Neilson to Jarrett, 1 November 1922, MCJ Papers.

37. F. S. Chapin to Jarrett, 28 January 1924, MCJ Papers.

38. Noted on letter of W. A. Neilson to Jarrett, 1 November 1922, MCJ Papers.

39. F. S. Chapin to Jarrett, 28 January 1924, MCJ Papers.

40. Ora M. Lewis to Mary van Kleeck, 4 August 1922, MvK Papers.

41. Edna Foley to E. Kimball, 21 September 1922, MvK Papers.

42. See E. Kimball to van Kleeck, 17 May 1922, MvK Papers. See also E. Kimball to Edna Foley, 23 September 1922, MvK Papers.

43. Dewson, interview, 22 July 1978; Cook, interview, 22 July 1978.

44. Bertha C. Reynolds, interview by Vida S. Grayson, January 1976, Social Work Archive of the Sophia Smith Collection, Smith College, Northampton, Mass.

45. Cook, interview, 22 July 1978.

46. Ora M. Lewis to van Kleeck, 4 August 1922, MvK Papers; Edna Foley to E. Kimball, 21 September 1922, MvK Papers; "van Kleeck" in *NAM: MP,* 707–709.

47. Vida Grayson, who has recorded a substantial amount of oral history on the Smith College School for Social Work, has pointed out to us that Jarrett was clearly a person of outstanding intelligence, but one who had made many enemies. Her reputation as a teacher was certainly not uniformly bad.

Several early students remembered Jarrett very positively. Conversation with Vida Grayson, 20 November 1984, Northampton, Mass.

48. Maida H. Solomon to Jarrett, n.d., MCJ Papers.

49. Ibid.

50. Ibid.

51. Herman Adler, Institute for Juvenile Research, Illinois Department of Public Welfare, to Jarrett, 28 September 1923, MCJ Papers.

52. Jarrett, Curriculum Vitae, MCJ Papers.

53. Reynolds, Informal Autobiography, 4–8, BCR Papers.

54. Ibid., 10.

55. Ibid., 14, emphasis in the original.

56. Ibid., 14–15.

57. Ibid., 16.

58. Ibid., 19.

59. Ibid., 24, emphasis in the original.

60. Ibid. For a discussion of these tensions in the 1930s see Ehrenreich, *Altruistic Imagination,* esp. 117–119.

61. Reynolds, Informal Autobiography, 34, BCR Papers.

62. Ibid., 35.

63. Ibid.

64. Schwartz, "Bertha Reynolds."

65. Reynolds, Informal Autobiography, 40, BCR Papers.

66. Ibid., 43.

67. Ibid., 112.

68. Ibid.

69. Lubove, *Professional Altruist,* 29–30.

70. Southard, "Lay Reaction to Psychiatry," 6.

71. Ibid.

72. Jill Conway, "Coeducation and Women's Studies: Two Approaches to the Question of Women's Place in the Contemporary University," *Daedalus* (Fall 1974): 243–244, discusses this general strategy among educated women beginning in the late nineteenth century.

73. By late 1970s 67 to 80 percent of social workers had no M.S.W. See David Wagner and Marcia Cohen, "Social Workers, Class, and Professionalism," *Catalyst* 1 (1978): 25–55, reprinted in *Social Structure and Social Work,* Smith College School for Social Work Anthology, Course 360, 1984–1985 (Lexington, Mass.: Ginn Custom Publishing, 1985), 312.

74. Magali Larson, *The Rise of Professionalism* (Berkeley: University of California Press, 1977), 31–34.

75. Ibid., 221. For scholars' treatment of them as "semi-professions" see Amitai Etzioni, ed., *The Semi-Professions and Their Organization* (New York: Free Press, 1969); Howard M. Vollmer and Donald L. Mills, ed., *Professionalization* (Englewood Cliffs, N.J.: Prentice-Hall, 1966).

76. R. L. Simpson and I. H. Simpson, "Women and Bureaucracy in the Semi-Professions," in *The Semi-Professions,* ed. Etzioni, 224; James W. Grimm, "Women in Female Dominated Professions," in *Women Working,* ed. A. H. Stromberg and S. Harkess (Palo Alto, Calif.: Mayfield, 1978), 293–315.

## Six. A View from the Margins

1. Josephine Baker, *Fighting for Life* (New York: Macmillan, 1939), 49–50.

2. Anne Walter Fearn, *My Days of Strength: An American Woman Doctor's Forty Years in China* (New York: Macmillan, 1939), 92–94, 98.

3. Alice Hamilton, *Exploring the Dangerous Trades* (Boston: Little, Brown, 1943), 119–125.

4. Deborah J. Warner, "Women Astronomers," *Natural History,* May 1979, 12–20.

5. Ibid., 14.

6. Mount Holyoke College, President, Report 1919–1920, 8, MHCL/A.

7. Warner, "Women Astronomers," 13–14.

8. Ibid., 14.

9. Barbara Melosh, *The Physicians Hand: Work, Culture, and Conflict in American Nursing* (Philadelphia: Temple University Press, 1982), 129.

10. See, for example, John P. Rousmaniere, "Cultural Hybrid in the Slums: The College Woman and the Settlement House, 1889–1894," *American Quarterly* 22 (Spring 1970): 45–66; Allen F. Davis, *Spearheads of Reform: The Social Settlement and the Progressive Movement* (New York: Oxford University Press, 1967).

11. Hamilton, *Exploring*, 115.

12. Ibid., 122–128.

13. Baker, *Fighting for Life*, 83–84, 114–115, chap. 7.

14. Viola Barnes, *Mount Holyoke in the Twentieth Century, 1971–72*, Oral History Interviews, transcripts, MHCL/A. The number of Ph.D.s on the faculty rose continually throughout Woolley's administration. Helen L. Horowitz points out that by 1911 the faculty had thirty-four Ph.D.s out of ninety members. See Horowitz, *Alma Mater: Design and Experience in the Women's Colleges from Their Nineteenth-Century Beginnings to the 1930s* (New York: Alfred A. Knopf, 1984), 233. For other books and articles about the women's colleges, see Barbara Solomon, *In the Company of Educated Women* (New Haven: Yale University Press, 1985); Roberta Frankfort, *College Women: Domesticity and Career in Turn of the Century America* (New York: New York University Press, 1977); Patricia A. Graham, "Expansion and Exclusion: A History of Women in American Higher Education," *Signs* 3 (Summer 1978): 759–773; M. Elizabeth Tidball, "Perspective on Academic Women and Affirmative Action," *Educational Record* 54 (Spring 1973): 130–135; Mary J. Oates and Susan Williamson, "Women's Colleges and Women Achievers," *Signs* 3 (Summer 1978): 795–806; Mabel Newcomer, *A Century of Higher Education for Women* (New York: Harper, 1959).

15. Anna Mary Wells, *Miss Marks and Miss Woolley* (Boston: Houghton Mifflin, 1978), chaps. 6–8, 11.

16. Mount Holyoke College, President, Inaugural Address 1901, 10–14, MHCL/A; also see, for example, Report to Mount Holyoke Board of Trustees, November 1911, which summarizes the first decade of her administration, MHCL/A; also President, Report 1919–1920, esp. 6, MHCL/A.

17. Ellen Deborah Ellis, *Mount Holyoke in the Twentieth Century, 1971–72,* Oral History Interviews, transcripts, MHCL/A.

18. Burton Bledstein, *The Culture of Professionalism* (New York: W. W. Norton, 1986), 282–286.

19. Jerold S. Auerbach, *Unequal Justice* (New York: Oxford University Press, 1976), 54, 75, and chap. 3; Rosemary Stevens, *Medicine and the Public Interest* (New Haven: Yale University Press, 1971), 72.

20. Auerbach, *Unequal Justice,* 100.

21. One reformer, Alfred Z. Reed, even suggested that the profession formally institutionalize the already potent norm that lawyers be explicitly stratified "by the economic position of the client rather than by the nature of the professional service rendered." Ibid., 59.

22. Cynthia Fuchs Epstein, *Women in Law* (New York: Basic Books, 1981), 53.

23. Auerbach, *Unequal Justice,* 61.

24. There is not yet a full-length biography of Mary van Kleeck. See "van Kleeck," in *NAW: MP,* 707–709. This volume is also the best source for an overview of many of these accomplished women. In addition, see Edith Finch, *Carey Thomas of Bryn Mawr* (New York: Harper, 1947); Wells, *Miss Marks and Miss Woolley;* Barbara Harris, *Beyond Her Sphere: Women and Professions in American History* (Westport, Conn.: Greenwood Press, 1978); Mary Walsh, *Doctors Wanted: No Women Need Apply* (New Haven: Yale University Press, 1977).

25. Auerbach, *Unequal Justice,* 72.

26. Stevens, *Medicine and the Public Interest,* 72.

27. Dorothy Reed Mendenhall, Unpublished Autobiography (1939–1953), fldr. I, DRM Papers.

28. Regina Morantz, "Feminism, Professionalism, and Germs: A Study in the Thought of Mary Putnam Jacobi and Elizabeth Blackwell," *American Quarterly* 34 (winter 1982):459–478; also see Rosalind Rosenberg, *Beyond Separate Spheres: Intellectual Roots of Modern Feminism* (New Haven: Yale University Press, 1982), see esp. "Introduction," xvi, and 161–162.

29. In a contemporary study Rosabeth Kanter has clearly documented the need for a critical mass in order to avoid the impotence and distortion of tokenism. See Kanter, *Men and Women of the Corporation* (New York: Basic Books, 1977), 281–284; also see Judith Long Laws, "Work Aspirations of Women: False Leads and New Starts," in *Women and the Workplace,* ed. Martha Blaxall and Barbara Reagan (Chicago: University of Chicago Press, 1976), 33–49; Walsh, *Doctors Wanted,* chap. 9, esp. 280–281.

30. Edna Yost, *American Women of Science* (New York: J. B. Lippincott Co., 1943), 88.

31. Hamilton, *Exploring,* 253.

32. Simon Flexner and James Thomas Flexner, *William Henry Welch and the Heroic Age of American Medicine* (New York: Viking Press, 1941), 72–73, 112–113.

33. Wells, *Miss Marks and Miss Woolley,* chap. 11; Margaret Judson, *Breaking the Barrier* (New Brunswick, N.J.: Rutgers Univesity Press, 1984), 75–76; Horowitz, *Alma Mater,* 302–306.

34. Robert Wiebe, *The Search for Order* (New York: Hill and Wang, 1967), 145–155.

35. See Thomas Haskell, *The Emergence of Professional Social Science* (Urbana: University of Illinois Press, 1977); Magali Larson, *The Rise of Professionalism* (Berkeley: University of California Press, 1977); H. Jamous and B. Peloille, "Professions or Self-Perpetuating Systems: Change in the French University Hospital System," in *Professions and Professional-*

*ization,* ed. J. A. Jackson (Cambridge: Cambridge University Press, 1970), 111–152.

36. Roy Lubove, *The Professional Altruist* (Cambridge: Harvard University Press, 1965), 83–84.

37. Alan Trachtenberg, *The Incorporation of America* (New York: Hill and Wang, 1982), 63–69; also Wiebe, *Search for Order,* 154–55.

38. Jamous and Peloille, "Professions or Self-Perpetuating Systems," esp. 140–141.

39. Mendenhall, Unpublished Autobiography, fldr. I, DRM Papers.

40. Kanter, *Men and Women of the Corporation,* 47–50.

41. Patricia M. Hummer, *The Decade of Elusive Promise: Professional Women in the United States, 1920–1930* (Ann Arbor, Mich.: UMI Research Press, 1979), chap. 6; William H. Chafe, *The American Woman* (New York: Oxford University Press, 1972), chaps. 2, 4; Lois Schaarf, *To Work and to Wed* (Westport, Conn.: Greenwood Press, 1980).

42. Betty Friedan, *The Feminine Mystique* (New York: Dell, 1963), chap. 2; Ruth Schwartz Cowan, *More Work for Mother* (New York: Basic Books, 1983), 203–205.

43. Walsh, *Doctors Wanted,* 230–235; Cynthia Fuchs Epstein, *Woman's Place* (Berkeley: University of California Press, 1971), 60, 168; Athena Theodore, "The Professional Woman: Trends and Prospects," in *The Professional Woman,* ed. Athena Theodore (Cambridge: Schenkman Publishing, 1971), 3.

44. Debra R. Kaufman, "Professional Women: How Real Are the Recent Gains?" in *Women: A Feminist Perspective,* 3d ed., ed. Jo Freeman (Palo Alto, Calif.: Mayfield Publishing, 1984), 353–369.

Poisons, Hamilton's research and industrial, 122, 149, 150–152, 153
Political issues: Hamilton and, 152, 158; Reynolds and, 196, 197
Prejudice. *See* Barriers to professions; Discrimination
"Prenatal and Natal Conditions in Wisconsin" (Reed), 98
Prentiss, Elizabeth, 43–49
Professional scholars. *See* Academics
Professionalism, defined, 2–3
Professions: changes in modern society and, 2–4; competition and, 217–218; concept of female frailty and, 82–93; contrasting men and women and, 234; development of psychiatric social work and, 166–170, 173–176, 199–203, 203–208; educational restructuring and, 224; homogeneous colleagues and, 239–240; marriage and, 17–18, 58; men's values and women in, 87; middle class women and, 3, 4, 13, 14; post-Civil War period and, 4–5; problem of being female in, 74–75; scholarly continuum concept in education and, 161–162, 231–235; scientific research as, 124, 127–128; situation of women in early, 14; unequal colleagues in, 144; visibility

and vulnerability of women in, 232–233; women pathfinders in, 9–13; women's aspirations and, 1–2, 143; women's careers in, 1. *See also* Barriers to professions
Progeny, problem of, 231–235
Psychiatric social work: development as a new specialty for women, 165–167; diagnoses of (Flexner), 173–176; graduate curriculum at Smith and, 176–191; graduate program at Smith and, 203–208; inability to achieve equal professional status in, 167–170; Reynolds and, 191–199; Smith's programs and, 170–173; study analysis and, 20–21; subordination and, 215; women's career development in, 199–203. *See also* Jarrett, Mary C.
Psychiatric Social Workers Club, 183
Public health: Baker and, 86, 100–101; Reed's work in, 97–100, 102–103; Sabin and, 122, 130, 136, 137
Public service. *See* Service concept
Putnam, Bertha, 9, 54, 66, 227; Mount Holyoke faculty and, 45–46, 49; scholarship and, 15

Red Cross, 182, 184
Reed, Dorothy, 5, 9, 16–18,